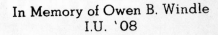

The Autobiography

OF
CALVIN COOLIDGE

CALVIN COOLIDGE

The Autobiography

OF

CALVIN COOLIDGE

New York
COSMOPOLITAN BOOK CORPORATION
1929

PRINTED IN THE U. S. A. BY
J. J. LITTLE & IVES CO., NEW YORK

CONTENTS

ILLUSTRATIONS

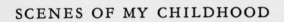

SCENES OF MY CHILDHOOD

CHAPTER ONE

SCENES OF MY CHILDHOOD

THE town of Plymouth lies on the easterly slope of the Green Mountains, about twenty miles west of the Connecticut River and somewhat south of the central part of Vermont. This part of the state is made up of a series of narrow valleys and high hills, some of which rank as mountains that must reach an elevation of at least twenty-five hundred feet.

Its westerly boundary is along the summit of the main range to where it falls off into the watershed of Lake Champlain and the St. Lawrence River. At one point a little rill comes down a mountain until it strikes a rock, where it divides, part running north into the Ottauquechee and part south into the Black River, both of which later turn easterly to reach the Connecticut.

In its natural state this territory was all covered

with evergreen and hardwood trees. It had large deposits of limestone, occasionally mixed with marble, and some granite. There were sporadic outcroppings of iron ore, and the sands of some of the streams showed considerable traces of gold. The soil was hard and rocky, but when cultivated supported a good growth of vegetation.

During colonial times this region lay in an unbroken wilderness, until the coming of the French and Indian War, when a military road was cut through under the direction of General Amherst, running from Charlestown, New Hampshire, to Fort Ticonderoga, New York. This line of march lay through the south part of the town, crossing the Black River at the head of the two beautiful lakes and running over the hill towards the valley of the Otter Creek.

When settlers began to come in around the time of the Revolution, the grandfather of my grandfather, Captain John Coolidge, located a farm near the height of land westward from the river along this military road, where he settled in about 1780.

He had served in the Revolutionary army and

[4]

may have learned of this region from some of his comrades who had known it in the old French wars, or who had passed over it in the campaign against Burgoyne, which culminated at Saratoga.

He had five children and acquired five farms, so that each of his descendants was provided with a homestead. His oldest son Calvin came into possession of the one which I now own, where it is said that Captain John spent his declining years. He lies buried beside his wife in the little neighborhood cemetery not far distant.

The early settlers of Plymouth appear to have come mostly from Massachusetts, though some of them had stopped on the way in New Hampshire. They were English Puritan stock, and their choice of a habitation stamps them with a courageous pioneering spirit.

Their first buildings were log houses, the remains of which were visible in some places in my early boyhood, though they had long since been given over to the sheltering of domestic animals. The town must have settled up with considerable rapidity, for as early as 1840 it had about fourteen hundred in-

[5]

habitants scattered about the valleys and on the sides of the hills, which the mountains divided into a considerable number of different neighborhoods, each with a well-developed local community spirit.

As time went on, much land was cleared of forest, very substantial buildings of wood construction were erected, saw mills and grist mills were located along the streams, and the sale of lumber and lime, farm products and domestic animals, brought considerable money into the town, which was laid out for improvements or found its way into the country store. It was a hard but wholesome life, under which the people suffered many privations and enjoyed many advantages, without any clear realization of the existence of either one of them.

They were a hardy self-contained people. Most of them are gone now and their old homesteads are reverting to the wilderness. They went forth to conquer where the trees were thicker, the fields larger, and the problems more difficult. I have seen their descendants scattered all over the country, especially in the middle west, and as far south as the Gulf of Mexico and westward to the Pacific slope.

[6]

It was into this community that I was born on the 4th day of July, 1872. My parents then lived in a five room, story and a half cottage attached to the post office and general store, of which my father was the proprietor. While they intended to name me for my father, they always called me Calvin, so the John became discarded.

Our house was well shaded with maple trees and had a yard in front enclosed with a picket fence, in which grew a mountain ash, a plum tree, and the customary purple lilac bushes. In the summertime my mother planted her flower bed there.

Her parents, who were prosperous farmers, lived in the large house across the road, which had been built for a hotel and still has the old hall in it where public dances were held in former days and a spacious corner on the front side known as the bar room, indicating what had been sold there before my grandfather Moor bought the premises. On an adjoining farm, about sixty-five rods distant, lived my grandfather and grandmother Coolidge. Within view were two more collections of farm buildings, three dwelling houses with their barns, a church, a school house and a blacksmith shop. A little out of sight dwelt the local butter tub maker and beyond him the shoemaker.

This locality was known as The Notch, being situated at the head of a valley in an irregular bowl of hills. The scene was one of much natural beauty, of which I think the inhabitants had little realization, though they all loved it because it was their home and were always ready to contend that it surpassed all the surrounding communities and compared favorably with any other place on earth.

My sister Abbie was born in the same house in April, 1875. We lived there until 1876, when the place was bought across the road, which had about two acres of land with a house and a number of barns and a blacksmith shop. About it were a considerable number of good apple trees. I think the price paid was $375. Almost at once the principal barn was sold for $100, to be moved away. My father was a good trader.

Some repairs were made on the inside, and black walnut furniture was brought from Boston to furnish the parlor and sitting room. It was a plain square-sided house with a long ell, to which the horse barn was soon added. The outside has since been remodeled and the piazza built. A young woman was always employed to do the house work. Whatever was needed never failed to be provided.

While in theory I was always urged to work and to save, in practice I was permitted to do my share of playing and wasting. My playthings often lay in the road to be run over, and my ball game often interfered with my filling the wood box. I have been taken out of bed to do penance for such derelictions.

My father, John Calvin Coolidge, ran the country store. He was successful. The annual rent of the whole place was $40. I have heard him say that his merchandise bills were about $10,000 yearly. He had no other expenses. His profits were about $100 per month on the average, so he must have sold on a very close margin.

He trusted nearly everybody, but lost a surprisingly small amount. Sometimes people he had not seen for years would return and pay him the whole bill.

He went to Boston in the spring and fall to buy

[9]

goods. He took the midnight train from Ludlow when they did not have sleeping cars, arriving in the city early in the morning, which saved him his hotel bill.

He was a good business man, a very hard worker, and did not like to see things wasted. He kept the store about thirteen years and sold it to my mother's brother, who became a prosperous merchant.

In addition to his business ability my father was very skillful with his hands. He worked with a carriage maker for a short time when he was young, and the best buggy he had for twenty years was one he made himself. He had a complete set of tools, ample to do all kinds of building and carpenter work. He knew how to lay bricks and was an excellent stone mason.

Following his sale of the store about the time my grandfather died, besides running the farm, he opened the old blacksmith shop which stood upon the place across the road to which we had moved. He hired a blacksmith at $1 per day, who was a large-framed powerful man with a black beard, said to be sometimes quarrelsome.

I have seen him unaided throw a refractory horse to the ground when it objected to being shod. But he was always kind to me, letting me fuss around the shop, leaving his own row to do three or four hills for me so that I could more easily keep up with the rest of the men in hoeing time, or favoring me in some way in the hay field as he helped on the farm in busy times.

He always pitched the hay on to the ox cart and I raked after. If I was getting behind he slowed up a little. He was a big-hearted man. I wish I could see that blacksmith again. The iron work for farm wagons and sleds was fashioned and put on in the shop, oxen and horses brought there for shoeing, and metal parts of farm implements often repaired. My father seemed to like to work in the shop, but did not go there much except when a difficult piece of work was required, like welding a broken steel section rod of a mowing machine, which had to be done with great precision or it would break again.

He kept tools for mending shoes and harnesses and repairing water pipes and tinware. He knew how to perform all kinds of delicate operations on

[11]

domestic animals. The lines he laid out were true and straight, and the curves regular. The work he did endured.

If there was any physical requirement of country life which he could not perform, I do not know what it was. From watching him and assisting him, I gained an intimate knowledge of all this kind of work.

It seems impossible that any man could adequately describe his mother. I can not describe mine.

On the side of her father, Hiram Dunlap Moor, she was Scotch with a mixture of Welsh and English. Her mother, Abigail (Franklin) Moor, was chiefly of the old New England stock. She bore the name of two Empresses, Victoria Josephine. She was of a very light and fair complexion with a rich growth of brown hair that had a glint of gold in it. Her hands and features were regular and finely modeled. The older people always told me how beautiful she was in her youth.

She was practically an invalid ever after I could remember her, but used what strength she had in lavish care upon me and my sister, who was three years younger. There was a touch of mysticism and poetry in her nature which made her love to gaze at the purple sunsets and watch the evening stars.

Whatever was grand and beautiful in form and color attracted her. It seemed as though the rich green tints of the foliage and the blossoms of the flowers came for her in the springtime, and in the autumn it was for her that the mountain sides were struck with crimson and with gold.

When she knew that her end was near she called us children to her bedside, where we knelt down to receive her final parting blessing.

In an hour she was gone. It was her thirty-ninth birthday. I was twelve years old. We laid her away in the blustering snows of March. The greatest grief that can come to a boy came to me. Life was never to seem the same again.

Five years and forty-one years later almost to a day my sister and my father followed her. It always seemed to me that the boy I lost was her image. They all rest together on the sheltered hillside among five generations of the Coolidge family.

My grandfather, Calvin Galusha Coolidge, died

when I was six years old. He was a spare man over six feet tall, of a nature which caused people to confide in him, and of a character which made him a constant choice for public office. His mother and her family showed a marked trace of Indian blood. I never saw her, but he took me one time to see her sister, his very aged aunt, whom we found sitting in the chimney corner smoking a clay pipe.

This was so uncommon that I always remembered it. I thought tobacco was only for men, though I had seen old ladies outside our neighborhood buy snuff at the store.

He was an expert horseman and loved to raise colts and puppies. He kept peacocks and other gay-colored fowl and had a yard and garden filled with scarlet flowers. But he never cared to hunt or fish. He found great amusement in practical jokes and could entice a man into a nest of bees and make him think he went there of his own accord.

He and my grandmother brought up as their own children the boy and girl of his only sister, whose parents died when they were less than two years old. He made them no charge, but managed their inheritance and turned it all over to them with the income, besides giving the boy $800 of his own money when he was eighteen years old, the same as he did my father. He was fond of riding horseback and taught me to ride standing up behind him. Some of the horses he bred and sold became famous. In his mind, the only real, respectable way to get a living was from tilling the soil. He therefore did not exactly approve having his son go into trade.

In order to tie me to the land, in his last sickness he executed a deed to me for life of forty acres, called the Lime Kiln lot, on the west part of his farm, with the remainder to my lineal descendants, thinking that as I could not sell it, and my creditors could not get it, it would be necessary for me to cultivate it. He also gave me a mare colt and a heifer calf, which came of stock that had belonged to his grandfather.

Two days after I was two months old, my father was elected to the state legislature. By a curious coincidence, when my son was the same age I was elected to the same office in Massachusetts. He was reelected twice, the term being two years, and, while

[15]

he was serving, my grandfather took my mother and me to visit him at Montpelier.

I think I was three years and four months old, but I always remembered the experience. Grandfather carried me to the State House and sat me in the Governor's chair, which did not impress me so much as a stuffed catamount that was in the capital museum. That was the first of the great many journeys which I have since made to legislative halls.

During his last illness he would have me read to him the first chapter of the Gospel of John, which he had read to his grandfather. I could do very well until I came to the word "comprehended," with which I always had difficulty. On taking the oath as President in 1925, I placed my hand on that Book of the Bible in memory of my first reading it.

So far as I know, neither he nor any other members of my family ever entertained any ambitions in my behalf. He evidently wished me to stay on the land. My own wish was to keep store, as my father had done.

They all taught me to be faithful over a few things. If they had any idea that such a training might some day make me a ruler over many things, it was not disclosed to me. It was my father in later years who wished me to enter the law, but when I finally left home for that purpose the parting was very hard for him to bear.

The neighborhood around The Notch was made up of people of exemplary habits. Their speech was clean and their lives were above reproach. They had no mortgages on their farms. If any debts were contracted they were promptly paid. Credit was good and there was money in the savings bank.

The break of day saw them stirring. Their industry continued until twilight. They kept up no church organization, and as there was little regular preaching the outward manifestation of religion through public profession had little opportunity, but they were without exception a people of faith and charity and of good works. They cherished the teachings of the Bible and sought to live in accordance with its precepts.

The conduct of the young people was modest and respectful. For most of the time during my boyhood regular Sunday school classes were held in the

[17]

church which my grandmother Coolidge superintended until in her advanced years she was superseded by my father. She was a constant reader of the Bible and a devoted member of the church, who daily sought for divine guidance in prayer.

I stayed with her at the farm much of the time and she had much to do with shaping the thought of my early years. She had a benign influence over all who came in contact with her. The Puritan severity of her convictions was tempered by the sweetness of a womanly charity. There were none whom she ever knew that had not in some way benefited by her kindness.

Her maiden name was Sarah Almeda Brewer. When she married my grandfather she was twenty and he was twenty-eight years old. She was accustomed to tell me that from his experience and observations he had come to have great faith in good blood, and that he chose her for his wife not only because he loved her, but because her family, which he had seen for three generations, were people of ability and character.

While he would have looked upon rank as only

[18]

pretense, he looked upon merit with great respect. His judgment was vindicated by the fact that more of her kin folks than he could have realized had been and were to become people of merited distinction.

The prevailing dress in our neighborhood was that of the countryside. While my father wore a business suit with a white shirt, collar and cuffs, which he always kept clean, the men generally had colored shirts and outer garments of brown or blue drilling. But they all had good clothes for any important occasions.

I was clad in a gingham shirt with overalls in the summer, when I liked to go barefooted. In the winter these were changed for heavy wool garments and thick cowhide boots, which lasted a year.

My grandmother Coolidge spun woolen yarn, from which she knitted us stockings and mittens. I have seen her weave cloth, and when I was ten years old I had a frock which came from her loom. We had linen sheets and table cloths and woolen bed blankets, which she had spun and woven in earlier days. I have some of them now. My grandfather

Coolidge wore a blue woolen frock much of the time, which is a most convenient garment for that region. It is cut like a shirt, going on over the head, with flaps that reach to the knees.

When I went to visit the old home in later years I liked to wear the one he left, with some fine calf-skin boots about two sizes too large for me, which were made for him when he went to the Vermont legislature about 1858. When news pictures began to be taken of me there, I found that among the public this was generally supposed to be a makeup costume, which it was not, so I have since been obliged to forego the comfort of wearing it. In public life it is sometimes necessary in order to appear really natural to be actually artificial.

Perhaps some glimpse of these pictures may have caused an English writer to refer to me as a Vermont backwoodsman. I wonder if he describes his King as a Scotchman when he sees him in kilts.

To those of his country who remember that Burgoyne sent home a dispatch saying that the Green Mountains were the abode of the most warlike race on the continent, who hung like a thunder cloud on his left—which was fully borne out by what they helped to do to him at Bennington and Saratoga—I presume the term of Vermont backwoodsman still carries the implication of reproach. But in this country it is an appellation which from General Ethan Allen to Admiral George Dewey has not been without some distinction.

While the form of government under which the Plymouth people lived was that of a republic, it had a strong democratic trend. The smallest unit was then the school district. Early in my boyhood the women were given a vote on school questions in both the district and town meetings.

The district meeting was held in the evening at the school house each year. The officers were chosen and the rate of the school tax was fixed by popular vote. The board and room of the teacher for two-week periods was then assigned to the lowest bidders. The rates ran from about fifty cents each week in the summer to as high as $1.25 in the winter.

The town officers were chosen annually at the March meeting. Here again the rate of taxes was fixed by popular vote. The bonded debt was rather large, coming down, as I was told, from expenses during the war and the costs of reconstructing roads and bridges after the disastrous freshet of 1869.

The more substantial farmers wanted to raise a large tax to reduce the debt. I noticed my father did not vote on this subject and I inquired his reason. He said that while he could afford to pay a high rate, he did not wish to place so large a burden on those who were less able, and so was leaving them to make their own decision.

In those days there were about two hundred and fifty qualified voters, not over twenty-five of which were Democrats, and the rest Republicans. They had their spirited contests in their elections, but not along party lines.

One of the patriarchs of the town, who was a Democrat, served many years as Moderator by unanimous choice. He was a man of sound common sense and an excellent presiding officer, but without much book learning.

When he read that part of the call for the meeting which recited that it was to act "on the following questions, *viz.,*" he always read it "to act upon the following questions, *vizley.*" This caused him to be referred to at times by the irreverent as Old Vizley.

I was accustomed to carry apples and popcorn balls to the town meetings to sell, mainly because my grandmother said my father had done so when he was a boy, and I was exceedingly anxious to grow up to be like him.

On the even years in September came the Freemen's meeting. This was a state election, at which the town representative to the legislature was chosen. They also voted for county and state officers and for a Representative to the Congress, and on each fourth year for Presidential electors. I attended all of these meetings until I left home and followed them with interest for many of the succeeding years.

Careful provision was made for the administration of justice through local authorities. Those charged with petty crimes and misdemeanors were brought before one of the five Justices of the Peace, who had power to try and sentence with or without calling a jury. He also had a like jurisdiction in civil matters of a small amount.

The more important cases, criminal and civil, went to the County Court which sat in the neighboring town of Woodstock in May and December. My father was nearly all his life a Constable or a Deputy Sheriff, and sometimes both, with power to serve civil and criminal process, so that he arrested those charged with crime and brought them before the Justice for trial.

Unless it would keep me out of school, he would take me with him when attending before the local justices or when he went to the opening session of the County Court. Before him my grandfather had held the same positions, so that together they were the peace officers most of the time in our town for nearly seventy-five years.

In addition to this they often settled the estates of deceased persons and acted as guardian of minors. This business was transacted in the Probate Court, where I often went.

My father was at times a Justice of the Peace and always had a commission as notary public. This enabled him to take the acknowledgment of deeds, which he knew how to draw, and administer oaths necessary to pension papers which he filled out for old soldiers usually without charge, or to take affidavits required on any other instruments.

In my youth he was also always engaged in the transaction of all kinds of town business, being constantly elected for that purpose. He was painstaking, precise and very accurate, and had such wide experience that the lawyers of the region knew they could rely on him to serve papers in difficult cases and make returns that would be upheld by the courts.

This work gave him such a broad knowledge of the practical side of the law that people of the neighborhood were constantly seeking his advice, to which I always listened with great interest. He always counseled them to resist injustice and avoid unfair dealing, but to keep their agreements, meet their obligations and observe strict obedience to the law.

By reason of what I saw and heard in my early life, I came to have a good working knowledge of the practical side of government. I understood that it consisted of restraints which the people had imposed upon themselves in order to promote the common welfare.

As I went about with my father when he collected taxes, I knew that when taxes were laid some one had to work to earn the money to pay them. I saw that a public debt was a burden on all the people in a community, and while it was necessary to meet the needs of a disaster it cost much in interest and ought to be retired as soon as possible.

After the winter work of laying in a supply of wood had been done, the farm year began about the first of April with the opening of the maple-sugar season. This was the most interesting of all the farm operations to me.

With the coming of the first warm days we broke a road through the deep snow into the sugar lot, tapped the trees, set the buckets, and brought the sap to the sugar house, where in a heater and pans it was boiled down into syrup to be taken to the house for sugaring off. We made eight hundred to two thousand pounds, according to the season.

After that the fences had to be repaired where they had been broken down by the snow, the cattle turned out to pasture, and the spring planting done. Then came sheep-shearing time, which was followed by getting in the hay, harvesting and threshing of the grain, cutting and husking the corn, digging the potatoes and picking the apples. Just before Thanksgiving the poultry had to be dressed for market, and a little later the fattened hogs were butchered and the meat salted down. Early in the winter a beef creature was slaughtered.

The work of the farm was done by the oxen, except running the mowing machine and horse rake. I early learned to drive oxen and used to plow with them alone when I was twelve years old. Of course, there was the constant care of the domestic animals, the milking of the cows, and taking them to and from pasture, which was especially my responsibility.

We had husking bees, apple-paring bees and singing schools in the winter. There were parties for the young folks and an occasional dramatic exhibition by local talent. Not far away there were some public dances, which I was never permitted to attend.

Some time during the summer we usually went to the circus, often rising by three o'clock so as to get there early. In the autumn we visited the county fair. The holidays were all celebrated in some fashion.

[27]

Of course, the Fourth of July meant a great deal to me, because it was my birthday. The first one I can remember was when I was four years old. My father took me fishing in the meadow brook in the morning. I recall that I fell in the water, after which we had a heavy thundershower, so that we both came home very wet. Usually there was a picnic celebration on that day.

Thanksgiving was a feast day for family reunions at the home of the grandparents. Christmas was a sacrament observed with the exchange of gifts, when the stockings were hung, and the spruce tree was lighted in the symbol of Christian faith and love. While there was plenty of hard work, there was no lack of pleasurable diversion.

When the work was done for the day, it was customary to drop into the store to get the evening mail and exchange views on topics of interest. A few times I saw there Attorney General John G. Sargent with his father, who was a much respected man.

A number of those who came had followed Sheridan, been with Meade at Gettysburg, and served under Grant, but they seldom volunteered any information about it. They were not talkative and took their military service in a matter of fact way, not as anything to brag about but merely as something they did because it ought to be done.

They drew no class distinctions except towards those who assumed superior airs. Those they held in contempt. They held strongly to the doctrine of equality. Whenever the hired man or the hired girl wanted to go anywhere they were always understood to be entitled to my place in the wagon, in which case I remained at home. This gave me a very early training in democratic ideas and impressed upon me very forcibly the dignity and power, if not the superiority of labor.

It was all a fine atmosphere in which to raise a boy. As I look back on it I constantly think how clean it was. There was little about it that was artificial. It was all close to nature and in accordance with the ways of nature. The streams ran clear. The roads, the woods, the fields, the people — all were clean. Even when I try to divest it of the halo which I know always surrounds the past, I am unable to

[29]

create any other impression than that it was fresh and clean.

We had some books, but not many. Mother liked poetry and read some novels. Father had no taste for books, but always took and read a daily paper. My grandfather Moor read books and papers, so that he was a well-informed man.

My grandmother Coolidge liked books and besides a daily Chapter in the Bible read aloud to me "The Rangers or the Tory's Daughter" and "The Green Mountain Boys," which were both stories of the early settlers of Vermont during the Revolutionary period. She also had two volumes entitled "Washington and His Generals," and other biographies which I read myself at an early age with a great deal of interest.

At home there were numerous law books. In this way I grew up with a working knowledge of the foundations of my state and nation and a taste for history.

My education began with a set of blocks which had on them the Roman numerals and the letters of the alphabet. It is not yet finished. As I played with

Allison Spence

VICTORIA JOSEPHINE (MOOR) COOLIDGE
Mother of Calvin Coolidge, about the time her marriage

them and asked my mother what they were, I came to know them all when I was three years old. I started to school when I was five.

The little stone school house which had unpainted benches and desks wide enough to seat two was attended by about twenty-five scholars. Few, if any, of my teachers reached the standard now required by all public schools. They qualified by examination before the town superintendent. I first took this examination and passed it at the age of thirteen and my sister Abbie passed it and taught a term of school in a neighboring town when she was twelve years old.

My teachers were young women from neighboring communities, except sometimes when a man was employed for the winter term. They were all intelligent, of good character, and interested in their work. I do not feel that the quality of their instruction was in any way inferior. The common school subjects were taught, with grammar and United States history, so that when I was thirteen I had mastered them all and went to Black River Academy, at Ludlow.

That was one of the greatest events of my life.

[31]

The packing and preparation for it required more time and attention than collecting my belongings in preparation for leaving the White House. I counted the hours until it was time to go.

My whole outfit went easily into two small hand-bags, which lay on the straw in the back of the traverse sleigh beside the fatted calf that was starting to market. The winter snow lay on the ground. The weather was well below freezing. But in my eagerness these counted for nothing.

I was going where I would be mostly my own master. I was casting off what I thought was the drudgery of farm life, symbolized by the cowhide boots and every-day clothing which I was leaving behind, not realizing what a relief it would be to return to them in future years. I had on my best clothes and wore shoes with rubbers, because the village had sidewalks.

I did not know that there were mental and moral atmospheres more monotonous and more contaminating than anything in the physical atmosphere of country life. No one could have made me believe that I should never be so innocent or so happy again.

As we rounded the brow of the hill the first rays of the morning sun streamed over our backs and lighted up the glistening snow ahead. I was perfectly certain that I was traveling out of the darkness into the light.

We have much speculation over whether the city or the country is the better place to bring up boys. I am prejudiced in behalf of the country, but I should have to admit that much depends on the parents and the surrounding neighborhood. We felt the cold in winter and had many inconveniences, but we did not mind them because we supposed they were the inevitable burdens of existence.

It would be hard to imagine better surroundings for the development of a boy than those which I had. While a wider breadth of training and knowledge could have been presented to me, there was a daily contact with many new ideas, and the mind was given sufficient opportunity thoroughly to digest all that came to it.

Country life does not always have breadth, but it has depth. It is neither artificial nor superficial, but is kept close to the realities.

While I can think of many pleasures we did not have, and many niceties of culture with which we were unfamiliar, yet if I had the power to order my life anew I would not dare to change that period of it. If it did not afford me the best that there was, it abundantly provided the best that there was for me.

SEEKING AN EDUCATION

CHAPTER TWO

SEEKING AN EDUCATION

O NE of the sages of New England is re-ported to have declared that the education of a child should begin several generations before it is born. No doubt it does begin at a much earlier period and we enter life with a heritage that reaches back through the ages. But we do not choose our ancestors. When we come into the world the gate of gifts is closed behind us. We can do nothing about it. So far as each individual is concerned all he can do is to take the abilities he has and make the most of them. His power over the past is gone. His power over the future depends on what he does with himself in the present. If he wishes to live and pro-gress he must work.

During early childhood the inspiration for any-thing like mental discipline comes almost entirely from the outside. It is supplied by the parents and teachers. It was not until I left home in February of 1886 that I could say I had much thought of my own about getting an education. Thereafter I began to be more dependent on myself and assume more and more self-direction. What I studied was the result of my own choice. Instead of seeking to direct me, my father left me to decide. But when I had selected a course he was always solicitous to see that I diligently applied myself to it.

Going away to school was my first great adventure in life. I shall never forget the impression it made on me. It was so deep and remains so vivid that whenever I have started out on a new enterprise a like feeling always returns to me. It was the same when I went to college, when I left home to enter the law, when I began a public career in Boston, when I started for Washington to become Vice-President and finally when I was called to the White House. Going to the Academy meant a complete break with the past and entering a new and untried field, larger and more alluring than the past, among unknown scenes and unknown people.

In the spring of 1886 Black River Academy had

just celebrated its fiftieth anniversary. While it had some distinguished alumni, the great body of its former students were the hard-working, every-day people, that made the strength of rural New England. My father and mother and grandmother Coolidge had been there a few terms. While it had a charter of its own, and was independent of the public authorities, it was nevertheless part village high school. At its head was a principal, who had under him two women assistants. A red brick structure, built like a church, with an assembly room and a few recitation rooms made up its entire equipment, so that those who did not live at home boarded in private families about the town of Ludlow. The spring term began in midwinter in order that the girls could be out by the first Monday in May to teach a summer district school and the boys could get home for the season's work on the farm.

For the very few who were preparing for college a classical course was offered in Latin, Greek, history and mathematics, but most of the pupils kept to the Latin Scientific, and the English courses. The student body was about one hundred and twenty-five in number. During my first term I began algebra and finished grammar. For some reason I was attracted to civil government and took that. This was my first introduction to the Constitution of the United States. Although I was but thirteen years old the subject interested me exceedingly. The study of it which I then began has never ceased, and the more I study it the more I have come to admire it, realizing that no other document devised by the hand of man ever brought so much progress and happiness to humanity. The good it has wrought can never be measured.

It was not alone the school with its teachers, its students and courses of study that interested me, but also the village and its people. It all lay in a beautiful valley along the Black River supported on either side by high hills. The tradespeople all knew my father well and he had an intimate acquaintance with the lawyers. Very soon I too knew them all. The chief industry of the town was a woolen mill that always remained a mystery to me. But the lesser activity of the village was a cab shop. I worked there some on Saturdays, so I came to know how toys and baby wagons were made. It was my first acquaintance with the factory system, and my approach to it was that of a wage earner. As I was employed at piece work my wages depended on my own ability, skill and industry. It was a good training. I was beginning to find out what existence meant.

My real academy course began the next fall term when I started to study Latin. In a few weeks I broke my right arm but it did not keep me out of school more than two days. Latin was not difficult for me to translate, but I never became proficient in its composition. Although I continued it until my sophomore year at college the only part of all the course that I found of much interest was the orations of Cicero. These held my attention to such a degree that I translated some of them in later life.

When Greek was begun the next year I found it difficult. It is a language that requires real attention and close application. Among its rewards are the moving poetry of Homer, the marvelous orations of Demosthenes, and in after life an increased power of observation.

Besides the classics we had a course in rhetoric, some ancient history, and a little American literature. Plane geometry completed our mathematics. In the modern languages there was only French.

In some subjects I began with the class when it started to review and so did the work of a term in two weeks. I joined the French class in mid year and made up the work by starting my study at about three o'clock in the morning.

During the long vacations from May until September I went home and worked on the farm. We had a number of horses so that I was able to indulge my pleasure in riding. As no one else in the neighborhood cared for this diversion I had to ride alone. But a horse is much company, and riding over the fields and along the country roads by himself, where nothing interrupts his seeing and thinking, is a good occupation for a boy. The silences of Nature have a discipline all their own.

Of course our school life was not free from pranks. The property of the townspeople was moved to strange places in the night. One morning as the janitor was starting the furnace he heard a loud bray from one of the class rooms. His investigation disclosed the presence there of a domestic animal noted

[42]

for his long ears and discordant voice. In some way during the night he had been stabled on the second floor. About as far as I deem it prudent to discuss my own connection with these escapades is to record that I was never convicted of any of them and so must be presumed innocent.

The expenses at the Academy were very moderate. The tuition was about seven dollars for each term, and board and room for each week not over three dollars. Oftentimes students hired a room for about fifty cents per week and boarded themselves. In my own case the cost for a school year averaged about one hundred and fifty dollars, which was all paid by my father. Any money I earned he had me put in the savings bank, because he wished me to be informed of the value of money at interest. He thought money invested in that way led to a self-respecting independence that was one of the foundations of good character.

It was about twelve miles from Ludlow to Plymouth. Sometimes I walked home Friday afternoon, but usually my father came for me and brought me back Sunday evening or Monday morning. When

[43]

this was not done I often staid with the elder sister of my mother, Mrs. Don C. Pollard, who lived about three miles down the river at Proctorsville. This was my Aunt Sarah who is still living. She was wonderfully kind to me and did all she could to take the place of my own mother in affection for me and good influence over me while I was at the Academy and ever after. The sweetness of her nature was a benediction to all who came in contact with her. What men owe to the love and help of good women can never be told.

The Academy had no athletics in those days, as the boys from the farms did not feel the need of such activity. A few games of baseball were played, but no football or track athletics were possible. Games did not interest me much though I had some skill with a bat. I was rather slender and not so tall as many boys of my age.

Those who attended the school from out of town were all there with a real purpose of improving themselves, so that while there was no lack of fun and play they all worked as best they could, for their coming had meant too much sacrifice at home not to be taken seriously. They had come seeking to better their condition in life through what they might learn and the self-discipline they might secure.

The school had much to be desired in organization and equipment, but it possessed a sturdy spirit and a wholesome regard for truth. Of course the student body came from the country and had country ways, but the boys were inspired with a purpose, and the girls with a sweet sincerity which becomes superior to all the affectations of the drawing-room. In them the native capacity for making real men and women remained all unspoiled.

The Presidential election of 1888 created considerable interest among the students. Most of them favored the Republican candidate Benjamin Harrison against the then President Grover Cleveland. When Harrison was elected, two nights were spent parading the streets with drums and trumpets, celebrating the victory.

During most of my course George Sherman was the principal and Miss M. Belle Chellis was the first assistant. I owe much to the inspiration and scholarly direction which they gave to my undergraduate

[45]

days. They both lived to see me President and sent me letters at the time, though they left the school long ago. It was under their teaching that I first learned of the glory and grandeur of the ancient civilization that grew up around the Mediterranean and in Mesopotamia. Under their guidance I beheld the marvels of old Babylon, I marched with the Ten Thousand of Xenophon, I witnessed the conflict around beleaguered Troy which doomed that proud city to pillage and to flames, I heard the tramp of the invincible legions of Rome, I saw the victorious galleys of the Eternal City carrying destruction to the Carthaginian shore, and I listened to the lofty eloquence of Cicero and the matchless imagery of Homer. They gave me a vision of the world when it was young and showed me how it grew. It seems to me that it is almost impossible for those who have not traveled that road to reach a very clear conception of what the world now means.

It was in this period that I learned something of the thread of events that ran from the Euphrates and the Nile through Athens to the Tiber and thence stretched on to the Seine and the Thames to be carried overseas to the James, the Charles and the Hudson. I found that the English language was generously compounded with Greek and Latin, which it was necessary to know if I was to understand my native tongue. I discovered that our ideas of democracy came from the agora of Greece, and our ideas of liberty came from the forum of Rome. Something of the sequence of history was revealed to me, so that I began to understand the significance of our own times and our own country.

In March of my senior year my sister Abbie died. She was three years my junior but so proficient in her studies that she was but two classes below me in school. She was ill scarcely a week. Several doctors were in attendance but could not save her. Thirty years later one of them told me he was convinced she had appendicitis, which was a disease not well understood in 1890. I went home when her condition became critical and staid beside her until she passed to join our mother. The memory of the charm of her presence and her dignified devotion to the right will always abide with me.

In the spring of 1890 came my graduation. The

class had five boys and four girls. With so small a number it was possible for all of us to take part in the final exercises with orations and essays. The subject that I undertook to discuss was "Oratory in History," in which I dealt briefly with the effect of the spoken word in determining human action.

It had been my thought, as I was but seventeen, to spend a year in some of the larger preparatory schools and then enter a university. But it was suddenly decided that a smaller college would be preferable, so I went to Amherst. On my way there I contracted a heavy cold, which grew worse, interfering with my examinations, and finally sent me home where I was ill for a considerable time.

But by early winter I was recovered, so that I did a good deal of work helping repair and paint the inside of the store building which my father still owned and rented. There was time for much reading and I gave great attention to the poems of Sir Walter Scott. After a few weeks in the late winter at my old school I went to St. Johnsbury Academy for the spring term. Its principal was Dr. Putney, who was a fine drill-master, a very exact scholar, and

Allison Spence

COLONEL JOHN C. COOLIDGE
While in the Vermont Senate

an excellent disciplinarian. He readily gave me a certificate entitling me to enter Amherst without further examination, which he would never have done if he had not been convinced I was a proficient student. His indorsement of the work I had already done, after having me in his own classes for a term, showed that Black River Academy was not without some merit.

During the summer vacation my father and I went to the dedication of the Bennington Battle Monument. It was a most elaborate ceremony with much oratory followed by a dinner and more speaking, with many bands of music and a long military parade. The public officials of Vermont and many from New York were there. I heard President Harrison, who was the first President I had ever seen, make an address. As I looked on him and realized that he personally represented the glory and dignity of the United States I wondered how it felt to bear so much responsibility and little thought I should ever know.

The fall of 1891 found me back at Amherst taking up my college course in earnest. Much of its social life centered around the fraternities, and although they did not leave me without an invitation to join them it was not until senior year that an opportunity came to belong to one that I wished to accept. It has been my observation in life that, if one will only exercise the patience to wait, his wants are likely to be filled.

My class was rather small, not numbering more than eighty-five in a student body of about four hundred. President Julius H. Seelye, who had led the college for about twenty years with great success as an educator and inspirer of young men, had just retired. He had been succeeded by President Merrill E. Gates, a man of brilliant intellect and fascinating personality though not the equal of his predecessor in directing college policy. But the faculty as a whole was excellent, having many strong men, and some who were preeminent in the educational field.

The college of that day had a very laudable desire to get students, and having admitted them, it was equally alert in striving to keep them and help them get an education, with the result that very few left of their own volition and almost none were dropped for failure in their work. There was no marked exodus at the first examination period, which was due not only to the attitude of the college but to the attitude of the students, who did not go there because they wished to experiment for a few months with college life and be able to say thereafter they had been in college, but went because they felt they had need of an education, and expected to work hard for that purpose until the course was finished. There were few triflers.

A small number became what we called sports, but they were not looked on with favor, and they have not survived. While the class has lost many excellent men besides, yet it seems to be true that unless men live right they die. Things are so ordered in this world that those who violate its law cannot escape the penalty. Nature is inexorable. If men do not follow the truth they cannot live.

My absence from home during my freshman year was more easy for me to bear because I was no longer leaving my father alone. Just before the opening of college he had married Miss Carrie A. Brown, who was one of the finest women of our neighborhood. I had known her all my life. After being without a mother nearly seven years I was greatly pleased to find in her all the motherly devotion that she could have given me if I had been her own son. She was a graduate of Kimball Union Academy and had taught school for some years. Loving books and music she was not only a mother to me but a teacher. For thirty years she watched over me and loved me, welcoming me when I went home, writing me often when I was away, and encouraging me in all my efforts. When at last she sank to rest she had seen me made Governor of Massachusetts and knew I was being considered for the Presidency.

It seems as though good influences had always been coming into my life. Perhaps I have been more fortunate in that respect than others. But while I am not disposed to minimize the amount of evil in the world I am convinced that the good predominates and that it is constantly all about us, ready for our service if only we will accept it.

In the Amherst College of my day a freshman was not regarded as different from the other classes.

He wore no distinctive garb, or emblem, and suffered no special indignities. It would not have been judicious for him to appear on the campus with a silk hat and cane, but as none of the other students resorted to that practice this single restriction was not a severe hardship. A cane rush always took place between the two lower classes very early in the fall term, but it was confined within the limits of good-natured sport, where little damage was done beyond a few torn clothes. If we had undertaken to have a class banquet where the sophomores could reach us, it undoubtedly would have brought on a collision, but when the time came for one we tactfully and silently departed for Westfield, under cover of a winter evening, where we were not found or molested.

It had long been the practice at Amherst to give careful attention to physical culture. It had, I believe, the first college gymnasium in this country. Each student on entering was given a thorough examination, furnished with a chart showing any bodily deficiencies and given personal direction for their removal. The attendance of the whole class was

[53]

required at the gymnasium drill for four periods each week, and voluntary work on the floor was always encouraged. We heard a great deal about a sound mind in a sound body.

At the time of my entrance the two college dormitories were so badly out of repair that they were little used. Later they were completely remodeled and became fully occupied. About ten fraternity houses furnished lodgings for most of the upper class men, but the lower class men roomed at private houses. All the students took their meals in private houses, so that there was a general comingling of all classes and all fraternities around the table, which broke up exclusive circles and increased college democracy.

The places of general assembly were for religious worship, which consisted of the chapel exercises at the first morning period each week day, and church service in the morning, with vespers in the late afternoon, on Sundays. Regular attendance at all of these was required. Of course we did not like to go and talked learnedly about the right of freedom of worship, and the bad mental and moral reactions from which we were likely to suffer as a result of being forced to hear scriptural readings, psalm singings, prayers and sermons. We were told that our choice of a college was optional, but that Amherst had been founded by pious men with the chief object of training students to overcome the unbelief which was then thought to be prevalent, that religious instruction was a part of the prescribed course, and that those who chose to remain would have to take it. If attendance on these religious services ever harmed any of the men of my time I have never been informed of it. The good it did I believe was infinite. Not the least of it was the discipline that resulted from having constantly to give some thought to things that young men would often prefer not to consider. If we did not have the privilege of doing what we wanted to do, we had the much greater benefit of doing what we ought to do. It broke down our selfishness, it conquered our resistance, it supplanted impulse, and finally it enthroned reason.

In intercollegiate athletics Amherst stood well. It won its share of trophies on the diamond, the gridiron and the track, but it did not engage in any of

the water sports. The games with Williams and
Dartmouth aroused the keenest interest, and honors.
were then about even. But these outside activities
were kept well within bounds and were not permitted to interfere with the real work of the college.
Pratt Field had just been completed and was well
equipped for outdoor sports, while Pratt Gymnasium had every facility for indoor training. These
places were well named, for the Pratt boys were very
active in athletics. One of them was usually captain
of the football team. I remember that in 1892
George D. Pratt, afterwards Conservation Commissioner of the State of New York, led his team to victory against Dartmouth, thirty to two, and a week
later kicked ten straight goals in a gale of wind at
the championship game with Williams, leaving the
score sixty to nothing in favor of Amherst. But both
these colleges have since retaliated with a great deal
of success.

In these field events I was only an observer, con-
tenting myself with getting exercise by faithful attendance at the class drills in the gymnasium. In
these the entire class worked together with dumb-

bells for most of the time, but they involved sufficient marching about the floor to give a military
flavor which I found very useful in later life when
I came in contact with military affairs during my
public career.

The Presidential election of 1892 came in my
sophomore year. I favored the renomination of Harrison and joined the Republican Club of the college,
which participated in a torch-light parade, but the
unsatisfactory business condition of the country carried the victory to Cleveland.

For nearly two years I continued my studies of
Latin and Greek. Ours was the last class that read
Demosthenes on the Crown with Professor William
S. Tyler, the head of the Greek department, who
had been with the college about sixty years. He was
a patriarch in appearance with a long beard and
flowing white hair.

His reverence for the ancient Greeks approached
a religion. It was illustrated by a story, perhaps
apocryphal, that one of his sons was sent to a theo-
logical school, and not wishing to engage in the min-
istry, wrote his father that the faculty of the school

[57]

held that Socrates was in hell. Such a reflection on the Greek philosopher so outraged the old man's loyalty that he wrote his son that the school was no place for him and directed him to come home at once.

In spite of his eighty-odd years he put the fire of youth into the translation of those glowing periods of the master orator, which were such eloquent appeals to the patriotism of the Greeks and such tremendous efforts to rouse them to the defense of their country. Those passages of the marvelous oration he said he had loved to read during the Civil War.

My studies of the ancient languages I supplemented with short courses in French, German and Italian.

But I never became very proficient in the languages. I was more successful at mathematics, which I pursued far enough to take calculus. This course was mostly under George D. Olds, who came to teach when we entered to study, which later caused us to adopt him as an honorary member of our class. In time he became President of the College. He had a peculiar power to make figures interesting and knew how to hold the attention and affection of his students. It was under him that we learned of the universal application of the laws of mathematics. We saw the discoveries of Kepler, Descartes, Newton and their associates bringing the entire universe under one law, so that the most distant point of light revealed by the largest reflector marches in harmony with our own planet. We discovered, too, that the same force that rounds a tear-drop holds all the myriad worlds of the universe in a balanced position. We found that we dwelt in the midst of a Unity which was all subject to the same rules of action. My education was making some headway.

In the development of every boy who is going to amount to anything there comes a time when he emerges from his immature ways and by the greater precision of his thought and action realizes that he has begun to find himself. Such a transition finally came to me. It was not accidental but the result of hard work. If I had permitted my failures, or what seemed to me at the time a lack of success, to discourage me I cannot see any way in which I would ever have made progress. If we keep our faith in ourselves, and what is even more important, keep our faith in regular and persistent application to hard work, we need not worry about the outcome.

During my first two years at Amherst I studied hard but my marks were only fair. It needed some encouragement from my father for me to continue. In junior year, however, my powers began to increase and my work began to improve. My studies became more interesting. I found the course in history under Professor Anson D. Morse was very absorbing. His lectures on medieval and modern Europe were inspiring, seeking to give his students not only the facts of past human experience but also their meaning. He was very strong on the political side of history, bringing before us the great figures from Charlemagne to Napoleon with remarkable distinctness, and showing us the influence of the Great Gregory and Innocent III. The work of Abélard and Erasmus was considered, and the important era of Luther and Calvin thoroughly explored.

In due time we crossed the Channel with William the Conqueror and learned how he subdued and solidified the Kingdom of England. The significance of the long struggle with the Crown before the Parliament finally reached a position of independence was disclosed, and the slow growth of a system of liberty under the law, until at last it was firmly established, was carefully explained. We saw the British Empire rise until it ruled the seas. The brilliance of the statesmanship of the different periods, the rugged character of the patriotic leaders, of Anselm and Simon de Montfort, of Cromwell and the Puritans, who dared to oppose the tyranny of the kings, the growth of learning, the development of commerce, the administration of justice— all these and more were presented for our consideration. Whatever was essential to a general comprehension of European history we had.

But it was when he turned to the United States that Professor Morse became most impressive. He placed particular emphasis on the era when our institutions had their beginning. Washington was treated with the greatest reverence, and a high estimate was placed on the statesmanlike qualities and financial capacity of Hamilton, but Jefferson was not neglected. In spite of his many vagaries it was shown that in saving the nation from the danger of falling under the domination of an oligarchy, and in establishing a firm rule of the people which was forever to remain, he vindicated the soundness of our political institutions. The whole course was a thesis on good citizenship and good government. Those who took it came to a clearer comprehension not only of their rights and liberties but of their duties and responsibilities.

The department of public speaking was under Professor Henry A. Frink. He had a strong hold on his students. His work went along with the other work, practically through the four years, beginning with composition and recitation and passing to the preparation and delivery of orations and participation in public debates. The allied subject of rhetoric I took under Professor John F. Genung, a scholarly man who was held in high respect. The courses in biology, chemistry, economics and geology I was not able to pursue, though they all interested me and were taught by excellent men.

Not the least in the educational values of Amherst was its beautiful physical surroundings. While the

college buildings of the early nineties were not impressive, the town with its spacious common and
fine elm trees was very attractive. It was located on
the arch of a slight ridge flanked on the north by
Mount Warner and on the south by the Holyoke
Range. The east rose over wooded slopes to the hori-
zon, and the west looked out across the meadows of
the Connecticut to the spires of Northampton and
the Hampshire Hills beyond. Henry Ward Beecher
has dwelt with great admiration and affection on
the beauties of this region, where he was a student.
Each autumn, when the foliage had put on its rich-
est tints, the College set aside Mountain Day to be
devoted to the contemplation of the scenery so wonderfully displayed in forest, hill, and dale, before
the frosts of winter laid them bare.

It always seemed to me that all our other studies
were in the nature of a preparation for the course
in philosophy. The head of this department was
Charles E. Garman, who was one of the most remarkable men with whom I ever came in contact.
He used numerous text books, which he furnished,
and many pamphlets that he not only had written

but had printed himself on a hand press in his home. These he pledged us to show to no one outside the class, because, being fragmentary, and disclosing but one line of argument which might be entirely demolished in succeeding lessons, they might involve him in some needless controversy. It is difficult to imagine his superior as an educator. Truly he drew men out.

Beginning in the spring of junior year his course extended through four terms. The first part was devoted to psychology, in order to find out the capacity and the limits of the human mind. It was here that we learned the nature of habits and the great advantage of making them our allies instead of our enemies.

Much stress was placed on a thorough mastery and careful analysis of all the arguments presented by the writers on any subject under consideration. Then when it was certain that they were fully understood they were criticized, so that what was unsound was rejected and what was true accepted. We were thoroughly drilled in the necessity of distinguishing between the accidental and the essential. The proper method of presenting a subject and an argument was discussed. We were not only learning about the human mind but learning how to use it, learning how to think. A problem would often be stated and the class left to attempt to find the solution unaided by the teacher. Above all we were taught to follow the truth whithersoever it might lead. We were warned that this would oftentimes be very difficult and result in much opposition, for there would be many who were not going that way, but if we pressed on steadfastly it was sure to yield the peaceable fruits of the mind. It does.

Our investigation revealed that man is endowed with reason, that the human mind has the power to weigh evidence, to distinguish between right and wrong and to know the truth. I should call this the central theme of his philosophy. While the quantity of the truth we know may be small it is the quality that is important. If we really know one truth the quality of our knowledge could not be surpassed by the Infinite.

We looked upon Garman as a man who walked with God. His course was a demonstration of the

[65]

existence of a personal God, of our power to know Him, of the Divine immanence, and of the complete dependence of all the universe on Him as the Creator and Father "in whom we live and move and have our being." Every reaction in the universe is a manifestation of His presence. Man was revealed as His son, and nature as the hem of His garment, while through a common Fatherhood we are all embraced in a common brotherhood. The spiritual appeal of music, sculpture, painting and all other art lies in the revelation it affords of the Divine beauty.

The conclusions which followed from this position were logical and inescapable. It sets man off in a separate kingdom from all the other creatures in the universe, and makes him a true son of God and a partaker of the Divine nature. This is the warrant for his freedom and the demonstration of his equality. It does not assume all are equal in degree but all are equal in kind. On that precept rests a foundation for democracy that cannot be shaken. It justifies faith in the people.

No doubt there are those who think they can demonstrate that this teaching was not correct. With

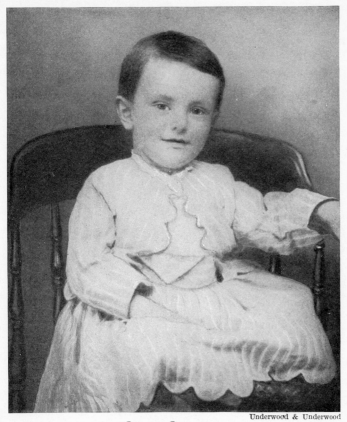

CALVIN COOLIDGE
At the age of three

them I have no argument. I know that in experience it has worked. In time of crisis my belief that people can know the truth, that when it is presented to them they must accept it, has saved me from many of the counsels of expediency. The spiritual nature of men has a power of its own that is manifest in every great emergency from Runnymede to Marston Moor, from the Declaration of Independence to the abolition of slavery.

In ethics he taught us that there is a standard of righteousness, that might does not make right, that the end does not justify the means and that expediency as a working principle is bound to fail. The only hope of perfecting human relationship is in accordance with the law of service under which men are not so solicitous about what they shall get as they are about what they shall give. Yet people are entitled to the rewards of their industry. What they earn is theirs, no matter how small or how great. But the possession of property carries the obligation to use it in a larger service. For a man not to recognize the truth, not to be obedient to law, not to render allegiance to the State, is for him to be at war with

[67]

his own nature, to commit suicide. That is why "the wages of sin is death." Unless we live rationally we perish, physically, mentally, spiritually.

A great deal of emphasis was placed on the necessity and dignity of work. Our talents are given us in order that we may serve ourselves and our fellow men. Work is the expression of intelligent action for a specified end. It is not industry, but idleness, that is degrading. All kinds of work from the most menial service to the most exalted station are alike honorable. One of the earliest mandates laid on the human race was to subdue the earth. That meant work.

If he was not in accord with some of the current teachings about religion, he gave to his class a foundation for the firmest religious convictions. He presented no mysteries or dogmas and never asked us to take a theory on faith, but supported every position by facts and logic. He believed in the Bible and constantly quoted it to illustrate his position. He divested religion and science of any conflict with each other, and showed that each rested on the common basis of our ability to know the truth.

To Garman was given a power which took his

class up into a high mountain of spiritual life and left them alone with God.

In him was no pride of opinion, no atom of self-ishness. He was a follower of the truth, a disciple of the Cross, who bore the infirmities of us all. Those who finished his course in the last term of senior year found in their graduating exercises a real commencement, when they would begin their efforts to serve their fellow men in the practical affairs of life. Of course it was not possible for us to accept immediately the results of his teachings or live altogether in accordance with them. I do not think he expected it. He was constantly reminding us that the spirit was willing but the flesh was *strong,* but that nevertheless, if we would continue steadfastly to think on these things we would be changed from glory to glory through increasing intellectual and moral power. He was right.

To many my report of his course will seem incomplete and crude. I am not writing a treatise but trying to tell what I secured from his teaching, and relating what has seemed important in it to me, from the memory I have retained of it, since I began

[69]

it thirty-five years ago. He expected it to be supplemented. He was fond of referring to it as a mansion not made with hands, incomplete, but sufficient for our spiritual habitation. What he revealed to us of the nature of God and man will stand. Against it "the gates of hell shall not prevail."

As I look back upon the college I am more and more impressed with the strength of its faculty, with their power for good. Perhaps it has men now with a broader preliminary training, though they then were profound scholars, perhaps it has men of keener intellects though they then were very exact in their reasoning, but the great distinguishing mark of all of them was that they were men of character. Their words carried conviction because we were compelled to believe in the men who uttered them. They had the power not merely to advise but literally to instruct their students.

In accordance with custom our class chose three of its members by popular vote to speak at the commencement. To me was assigned the grove oration, which according to immemorial practice deals with the record of the class in a witty and humorous way.

While my effort was not without some success I very soon learned that making fun of people in a public way was not a good method to secure friends, or likely to lead to much advancement, and I have scrupulously avoided it.

In the latter part of my course my scholarship had improved, so that I was graduated *cum laude*.

After my course was done I went home to do a summer's work on the farm, which was to be my last. I had decided to enter the law and expected to attend a law school, but one of my classmates wrote me late in the summer that there was an opportunity to go into the office of Hammond and Field at Northampton, so I applied to them and was accepted. After I had been there a few days a most courteous letter came from the Honorable William P. Dillingham requesting me to call on him at Montpelier and indicating he would take me into his office. He recalled the circumstance when I found him in the Senate after I became Vice President. But I had already reverted to Massachusetts, where my family had lived for one hundred and fifty years before their advent into Vermont. Had his letter reached me sooner probably it would have changed the whole course of my life.

Northampton was the county seat and a quiet but substantial town, with pleasant surroundings and fine old traditions reaching back beyond Jonathan Edwards. It was just recovering from the depression of 1893, preparing to eliminate its grade crossings and starting some new industries that would add to the business it secured from Smith College, which was a growing institution with many hundreds of students.

The senior member of the law firm was John C. Hammond, who was considered the leader of the Hampshire Bar. He was a lawyer of great learning and wide business experience, with a remarkable ability in the preparation of pleadings and an insight that soon brought him to the crucial point of a case. He was massive and strong rather than elegant, and placed great stress on accuracy. He presented a cause in court with ability and skill. The junior member was Henry P. Field, an able lawyer and a man of engaging personality and polish, who I found was an Alderman. That appeared to me at the time to be close to the Almighty in importance. I shall always remember with a great deal of gratitude the kindness of these two men to me.

That I was now engaged in the serious enterprise of life I so fully realized that I went to the barber shop and divested myself of the college fashion of long hair. Office hours were from eight to about six o'clock, during which I spent my time in reading Kent's Commentaries and in helping prepare writs, deeds, wills, and other documents. My evenings I gave to some of the masters of English composition. I read the speeches of Lord Erskine, of Webster, and Choate. The essays of Macaulay interested me much, and the writings of Carlyle and John Fiske I found very stimulating. Some of the orations of Cicero I translated, being especially attached to the defense of his friend the poet Archias, because in it he dwelt on the value and consolation of good literature. I read much in Milton and Shakespeare and found delight in the shorter poems of Kipling, Field and Riley.

My first Christmas was made more merry by getting notice that the Sons of the American Revolution had awarded me the prize of a gold medal worth about one hundred and fifty dollars for writing the best essay on "The Principles Fought for in the American Revolution," in a competition open to the seniors of all the colleges of the nation. The notice came one day, and it was announced in the next morning papers, where Judge Field saw it before I had a chance to tell him. So when he came to the office he asked me about it. I had not had time to send the news home. And then I had a little vanity in wishing my father to learn of it first from the press, which he did. He had questioned some whether I was really making anything of my education, in pretense I now think, not because he doubted it but because he wished to impress me with the desirability of demonstrating it.

But my main effort in those days was to learn the law. The Superior Court had three civil and two criminal terms each year in Northampton. Whenever it was sitting I spent all my time in the court room. In this way I became familiar with the practical side of trial work. I soon came to see that the counsel who knew the law were the ones who held the attention of the Judge, took the jury with them, and won their cases. They were prepared. The office where I was had a very large general practice which covered every field and took them into all the Courts of the Commonwealth but little into the Federal Courts. I assisted in the preparation of cases and went to court with the members of the firm to watch all their trial work and help keep a record of testimony for use in the arguments. It was all a work of absorbing interest to me.

The books in the office soon appeared too ponderous for my study, so I bought a supply of students' text books and law cases on the principal subjects necessary for my preparation for the bar. These enabled me to gain a more rapid acquaintance with the main legal principles, because I did not have to read through so much unimportant detail as was contained in the usual treatise prepared for a lawyer's library, which was usually a collection of all the authorities, while what I wanted was the main elements of the law. I was soon conversant with contracts, torts, evidence, and real property, with some knowledge of Massachusetts pleading, and had a considerable acquaintance with the practical side of statute law.

I do not feel that any one ever really masters the law, but it is not difficult to master the approaches to the law, so that given a certain state of facts it is possible to know how to marshal practically all the legal decisions which apply to them. I think counsel are mistaken in the facts of their case about as often as they are mistaken in the law.

All my waking hours were so fully employed that I found little time for play. My college was but eight miles distant, yet I did not have any desire to go back to the intercollegiate games, though I was accustomed to attend the alumni dinner at commencement. There was a canoe club which I joined, on the Connecticut, about a mile over the meadow from the town where I often went on Sunday afternoons. I was full of the joy of doing something in the world. Another reason why I discarded all outside enterprises and kept strictly to my work and my books was because I was keeping my monthly expenditures within thirty dollars which was furnished me by my father. He would gladly have provided me more had I needed it, but I thought that was enough and was determined to live within it, which I did. Not much was left for any unnecessary pleasantries of life.

Soon after I entered the office Mr. Hammond was elected District Attorney and Mr. Field became Mayor of the city, so that I saw something of the working of the city government and the administration of the criminal law.

The first summer I was in Northampton came the famous free silver campaign of 1896. When Mr. Bryan was nominated he had the support of most of the local Democrats of the city, but he lost much of it before November. One of them sent a long communication to a county paper indorsing him. This I answered in one of the city papers. When I was home that summer I took part in a small neighborhood debate in which I supported the gold standard. The study I put on this subject well repaid me. Of course Northampton went handsomely for McKinley.

With the exception of a week or two at home in the summer of 1896 I kept on in this way with my work from September, 1895, to June, 1897. I then felt sufficiently versed in the law to warrant my taking the examination for admission to the Bar. It was conducted by a County Committee of which Mr. Hammond was a member, but as I was his student he left the other two, Judge William G. Bassett and Judge William P. Strickland, to act on my petition. I was pronounced qualified by them and just before July 4, 1897, I was duly admitted to practice before the Courts of Massachusetts. My preparation had taken about twenty months. Only after I was finally in possession of my certificate did I notify my father. He had expected that my studies would take another year, and I wanted to surprise him if I succeeded and not disappoint him if I failed. I did not fail. I was just twenty-five years old and very happy.

It was a little over eleven years from the time I left home for the Academy in the late winter of 1886 until I was admitted to the Bar in the early summer of 1897. They had been years full of experience for me, in which I had advanced from a child to a man. Wherever I went I found good people, men and women, and young folks of my own age, who had won my respect and affection. From the hearthstone of my father's fireside to the court room at Northampton they had all been kind and helpful to me. Their memory will always be one of my most cherished possessions.

My formal period of education was passed, though my studies are still pursued. I was devoted to the law, its reasonableness appealed to my mind as the best method of securing justice between man and man. I fully expected to become the kind of country lawyer I saw all about me, spending my life in the profession, with perhaps a final place on the Bench. But it was decreed to be otherwise. Some Power that I little suspected in my student days took me in charge and carried me on from the obscure neighborhood at Plymouth Notch to the occupancy of the White House.

CHAPTER THREE

THE LAW AND POLITICS

THE LAW AND POLITICS

IT is one thing to know how to get admitted to the Bar but quite another thing to know how to practice law. Those who attend a law school know how to pass the examinations, while those who study in an office know how to apply their knowledge to actual practice. It seems to me that the best course is to go to a school and then go into an office where the practice is general. In that way the best preparation is secured for a thorough comprehension of the great basic principles of the profession and for their application to existing facts. Still, one who has had a good college training can do very well by starting in an office. But in any case he should not go into the law because it appears to be merely a means of making a living, but because he has a real and sincere love for the profession, which will enable him to make the sacrifices it requires.

When I decided to enter the law it was only natural, therefore, that I should consider it the highest of the professions. If I had not held that opinion it would have been a measure of intellectual dishonesty for me to take it for a life work. Others may be hampered by circumstances in making their choice, but I was free, and I went where I felt the duties would be congenial and the opportunities for service large. Those who follow other vocations ought to feel the same about them, and I hope they do.

My opinion had been formed by the high estimation in which the Bench and Bar were held by the people in my boyhood home in Vermont. It was confirmed by my more intimate intercourse with the members of the profession with whom I soon came in contact in Massachusetts after I went there to study law in the autumn of 1895. When I was admitted to practice two years later the law still occupied the high position of a profession. It had not then assumed any of its later aspects of a trade.

The ethics of the Northampton Bar were high. It was made up of men who had, and were entitled to have, the confidence and respect of their neighbors who knew them best. They put the interests of their clients above their own, and the public interests above them both. They were courteous and tolerant toward each other and respectful to the Court. This attitude was fostered by the appreciation of the uprightness and learning of the Judges.

Because of the short time I had spent in preparation I remained in the office of Hammond and Field about seven months after I was admitted to the Bar. I was looking about for a place to locate but found none that seemed better than Northampton. A new block called the Masonic Building was under construction on lower Main Street, and when it was ready for occupancy I opened an office there February 1, 1898. I had two rooms, where I was to continue to practice law for twenty-one years, until I became Governor of Massachusetts in 1919. For my office furniture and a good working library I paid about $800 from some money I had saved and inherited from my grandfather Moor. My rent was $200 per year. I began to be self-sustaining except as to the cost of my table board, which was paid by my father until September, but thereafter all my expenses I paid from the fees I received.

I was alone. While I had many acquaintances that I might call friends I had no influential supporters who were desirous to see me advanced and were sending business to me. I was dependent on the general public; what I had, came from them. My earnings for the first year were a little over $500.

My interest in public affairs had already caused me to become a member of the Republican City Committee, and in December, 1898, I was elected one of the three members of the Common Council from Ward Two. The office was without salary and not important, but the contacts were helpful. When the local military company returned that summer from the Cuban Campaign I did my best to get an armory built for them. I was not successful at that time but my proposal was adopted a little later. This was the beginning of an interest in military preparation which I have never relinquished.

During 1899 I began to get more business. The Nonotuck Savings Bank was started early that year, and I became its counsel. Its growth was slow but

steady. In later years I was its President, a purely
honorary place without salary but no small honor.
There was legal work about the county which came
to my office, so that my fees rose to $1,400 for the
second year.

I did not seek reelection to the City Council, as
I knew the City Solicitor was to retire and I wanted
that place. The salary was $600, which was not un-
important to me. But my whole thought was on my
profession. I wanted to be City Solicitor because I
believed it would make me a better lawyer. I was
elected and held the office until March, 1902. It
gave me a start in the law which I was ever after
able to hold.

The office was not burdensome and went along
with my private practice. It took me into Court
some. In a jury trial I lost two trifling cases in an
action of damages against the city for taking a small
strip of land to widen a highway. I felt I should
have won these cases on the claim that the land in
question already belonged to the highway. But I
prevailed in an unimportant case in the Supreme
Court against my old preceptor Mr. Hammond. It

[87]

is unnecessary to say that usually my cases with him were decided in his favor. The training in this office gave me a good grasp of municipal law, that later brought some important cases to me.

In addition to the mortgage and title work of the Savings Bank, I managed some real estate, and had considerable practice in the settlement of estates. Through a collection business I also had some insolvency practice. I recall an estate in Amherst and one in Belchertown, both much involved in litigation, which I settled. In each case Stephen S. Taft of Springfield was the opposing counsel. Perhaps there is no such thing as a best lawyer, any more than there is a best book, or a best picture, but to me Mr. Taft was the best lawyer I ever saw. If he was trying a case before a jury he was always the thirteenth juryman, and if the trial was before the court he was always advising the Judge. But he did not win these cases. He became one of my best friends, and we were on the same side in several cases in later years. One time he said to me: "Young man, when you can settle a case within reason you settle it. You will not make so large a fee out of some one case in that way, but at the end of the year you will have more money and your clients will be much better satisfied." This was sound advice and I heeded it. People began to feel that they could consult me with some safety and without the danger of being involved needlessly in long and costly litigation in court. Very few of my clients ever had to pay a bill of costs. I suppose they were more reasonable than other clients, for they usually settled their differences out of court. This course did not give me much experience in the trial of cases, so I never became very proficient in that art, but it brought me a very satisfactory practice and a fair income.

I worked hard during this early period. The matters on which I was engaged were numerous but did not involve large amounts of money and the fees were small. For three years I did not take the time to visit my old home in Vermont, but when I did go I was City Solicitor. My father began to see his hopes realized and felt that his efforts to give me an education were beginning to be rewarded.

What I always felt was the greatest compliment ever paid to my professional ability came in 1903.

[89]

In the late spring of that year William H. Clapp, who had been for many years the Clerk of the Courts for Hampshire County died. His ability, learning and painstaking industry made him rank very high as a lawyer. The position he held was of the first importance, for it involved keeping all the civil and criminal records of the Superior Court and the Supreme Judicial Court for the County. The Justices of the Supreme Judicial Court appointed me to fill the vacancy. I always felt this was a judgment by the highest Court in the Commonwealth on my professional qualifications. Had I been willing to accept the place permanently I should have been elected to it in the following November. The salary was then $2,300, and the position was one of great dignity, but I preferred to remain at the Bar, which might be more precarious, but also had more possibilities. Later events now known enable any one to pass judgment on my decision. Had I decided otherwise I could have had much more peace of mind in the last twenty-five years.

As the Clerk of the Courts I learned much relating to Massachusetts practice, so that ever after I

CALVIN COOLIDGE
At the age of seven

knew what to do with all the documents in a trial,
which would have been of much value to me if I had
not been called on to give so much time to political
affairs. These took up a large amount of my attention in 1904 after I went back to my office, so that
my income diminished during that year. I had been
chosen Chairman of the Republican City Committee. It was a time of perpetual motion in Massachusetts politics. The state elections came yearly in
November, and the city elections followed in December. This was presidential year. While I elected
the Representatives to the General Court by a comfortable margin at the state election I was not so successful in the city campaign. Our Mayor had served
three terms, which had always been the extreme
limit in Northampton, but he was nominated for a
fourth time. He was defeated by about eighty votes.
We made the mistake of talking too much about the
deficiencies of our opponents and not enough about
the merits of our own candidates. I have never
again fallen into that error. Feeling one year was all
I could give to the chairmanship I did not accept a
reelection but still remained on the committee.

My earnings had been such that I was able to make some small savings. My prospects appeared to be good. I had many friends and few enemies. There was a little more time for me to give to the amenities of life. I took my meals at Rahar's Inn where there was much agreeable company consisting of professional and business men of the town and some of the professors of Smith College. I had my rooms on Round Hill with the steward of the Clarke School for the Deaf. While these relations were most agreeable and entertaining I suppose I began to want a home of my own.

After she had finished her course at the University of Vermont Miss Grace Goodhue went to the Clarke School to take the training to enable her to teach the deaf. When she had been there a year or so I met her and often took her to places of entertainment.

In 1904 Northampton celebrated its two hundred and fiftieth anniversary. One evening was devoted to a reception for the Governor and his Council, given by the Daughters of the American Revolution. Miss Goodhue accompanied me to the City Hall where the reception was held, and after strolling around for a time we sat down in two comfortable vacant chairs. Soon a charming lady approached us and said that those chairs were reserved for the Governor and Mrs. Bates and that we should have to relinquish them, which we did. Fourteen years later when we had received sufficient of the election returns to show that I had been chosen Governor of Massachusetts I turned to her and said, "The Daughters of the American Revolution cannot put us out of the Governor's chair now."

From our being together we seemed naturally to come to care for each other. We became engaged in the early summer of 1905 and were married at her home in Burlington, Vermont, on October fourth of that year. I have seen so much fiction written on this subject that I may be pardoned for relating the plain facts. We thought we were made for each other. For almost a quarter of a century she has borne with my infirmities, and I have rejoiced in her graces.

After our return from a trip to Montreal we

[93]

staid a short time at the Norwood Hotel but soon started housekeeping. We rented a very comfortable house that needed but one maid to help Mrs. Coolidge do her work. Of course my expenses increased, and I had to plan very carefully for a time to live within my income. I know very well what it means to awake in the night and realize that the rent is coming due, wondering where the money is coming from with which to pay it. The only way I know of escape from that constant tragedy is to keep running expenses low enough so that something may be saved to meet the day when earnings may be small.

When the city election was approaching in December I was asked to be a candidate for School Committee. It was a purely honorary office, which had no attraction for me, but I consented and was nominated. To my surprise another Republican took out nomination papers, which split the party and elected a Democrat. The open compliment was that I had no children in the schools, but the real reason was that I was a politician. That reputation I had acquired by long service on the party committee helping elect our candidates. The man they elected gave a useful service for several years and left me free to turn to avenues which were to be much more useful to me in ways for public service. I was also better off attending to my law practice and my new home.

The days passed quietly with us until the next autumn, when we moved into the house in Massasoit Street that was to be our home for so long. I attended to the furnishing of it myself, and when it was ready Mrs. Coolidge and I walked over to it. In about two weeks our first boy came on the evening of September seventh. The fragrance of the clematis which covered the bay window filled the room like a benediction, where the mother lay with her baby. We called him John in honor of my father. It was all very wonderful to us.

We liked the house where our children came to us and the neighbors who were so kind. When we could have had a more pretentious home we still clung to it. So long as I lived there, I could be independent and serve the public without ever thinking that I could not maintain my position if I lost my office. I always made my living practicing law up to the time I became Governor, without being dependent on any official salary. This left me free to make my own decisions in accordance with what I thought was the public good. We lived where we did that I might better serve the people.

My main thought in those days was to improve myself in my profession. I was still studying law and literature. Because I thought the experience would contribute to this end I became a candidate for the Massachusetts House of Representatives. In a campaign in which I secured a large number of Democratic votes, many of which never thereafter deserted me, I was elected by a margin of about two hundred and sixty.

The Speaker assigned me to the Committees on Constitutional Amendments and Mercantile Affairs. During the session I helped draft, and the Committee reported, a bill to prevent large concerns from selling at a lower price in one locality than they did in others, for the purpose of injuring their competitor. This seemed to me an unfair trade practice that should be abolished. We secured the passage of the bill in the House, but the Senate rewrote it in such a way that it finally failed. I also supported a resolution favoring the direct election of United States Senators and another providing for woman suffrage. These measures did not have the approbation of the conservative element of my party, but I had all the assurance of youth and ignorance in supporting them, and later I saw them all become the law.

The next year I was reelected, but in running against a man who had a strong hold on some of the Republican Wards, my vote was cut down. Serving on the Judiciary Committee, which I wanted because I felt it would assist me in my profession, I became much interested in modifying the law so that an injunction could not be issued in a labor dispute to prevent one person seeking by argument to induce another to leave his employer. This bill failed. While I think it had merit, in later years I came to see that what was of real importance to the wage earners was not how they might conduct a quarrel with their employers, but how the business of the country might be so organized as to insure steady employment at a fair rate of pay. If that were done there would be no occasion for a quarrel, and if it were not done a quarrel would do no one any good.

The work in the General Court was fascinating, both from its nature and from the companionship with able and interesting men, but it took five days each week for nearly six months, so that I thought I had secured about all the benefit I could by serving two terms and declined again to be a candidate. Another boy had been given into our keeping April 13 who was named Calvin, so I had all the more reason for staying at home.

My law office took all my attention. I never had a retainer from any one, so my income always seemed precarious, but a practice which was general in its nature kept coming to me. In June of 1909 I went to Phoenix, Arizona, to hold a corporation meeting. It was the first I had seen of the West. The great possibilities of the region were apparent, and the enthusiasm of the people was inspiring. It told me that our country was sure to be a success.

For two years Northampton had elected a Democrat to be Mayor. He was a very substantial business man, who has since been my landlord for a long period. He was to retire, and the Republicans were anxious to elect his successor. At a party conference it was determined to ask me to run and I accepted the opportunity, thinking the honor would be one that would please my father, advance me in my profession, and enable me to be of some public service. It was a local office, not requiring enough time to interfere seriously with my own work.

Without in any way being conscious of what I was doing I then became committed to a course that was to make me the President of the Senate of Massachusetts and of the Senate of the United States, the second officer of the Commonwealth and the country, and the chief executive of a city, a state and a nation. I did not plan for it but it came. I tried to treat people as they treated me, which was much better than my deserts, in accordance with the precept of the master poet. By my studies and my course of life I meant to be ready to take advantage of opportunities. I was ready, from the time the Justices named me the Clerk of the Courts until my party nominated me for President.

Ever since I was in Amherst College I have remembered how Garman told his class in philosophy that if they would go along with events and have the courage and industry to hold to the main stream, without being washed ashore by the immaterial cross currents, they would some day be men of power. He meant that we should try to guide ourselves by general principles and not get lost in particulars. That may sound like mysticism, but it is only the mysticism that envelopes every great truth. One of the greatest mysteries in the world is the success that lies in conscientious work.

My first campaign for Mayor was very intense. My opponent was a popular merchant, a personal friend of mine who years later was to be Mayor, so that at the outset he was the favorite. The only issue was our general qualifications to conduct the business of the city. I called on many of the voters personally, sent out many letters, spoke at many ward rallies and kept my poise. In the end most of my old Democratic friends voted for me, and I won by about one hundred and sixty-five votes.

On the first Monday of January, 1910, I began a public career that was to continue until the first

Monday of March, 1929, when it was to end by my own volition.

Our city had always been fairly well governed and had no great problems. Taxes had been increasing. I was able to reduce them some and pay part of the debt, so that I left the net obligations chargeable to taxes at about $100,000. The salaries of teachers were increased. My work commended itself to the people, so that running against the same opponent for reelection my majority was much increased. I celebrated this event by taking my family to Montpelier where my father was serving in the Vermont Senate. Of all the honors that have come to me I still cherish in a very high place the confidence of my friends and neighbors in making me their Mayor.

Remaining in one office long did not appeal to me, for I was not seeking a public career. My heart was in the law. I thought a couple of terms in the Massachusetts Senate would be helpful to me, so when our Senator retired I sought his place in the fall of 1911 and was elected.

The winter in Boston I did not find very satisfactory. I was lonesome. My old friends in the House were gone. The Western Massachusetts Club that had its headquarters at the Adams House, where most of us lived that came from beyond the Connecticut, was inactive. The Committees I had, except the Chairmanship of Agriculture, did not interest me greatly, and to crown my discontent a Democratic Governor sent in a veto, which the Senate sustained, to a bill authorizing the New Haven Railroad to construct a trolley system in Western Massachusetts.

But as chairman of a special committee I had helped settle the Lawrence strike, secured the appointment of a commission that resulted in the passage of a mothers' aid or maternity bill at the next session, and I was made chairman of a recess committee to secure better transportation for rural communities in the western part of the Commonwealth.

During the summer we did a large amount of work on that committee and made a very full and constructive report at the opening of the General Court in 1913. This was the period that the Republican party was divided between Taft and Roosevelt, so that Massachusetts easily went for Wilson. But in the three-cornered contest I was reelected to the Senate.

It was in my second term in the Senate that I began to be a force in the Massachusetts Legislature. President Greenwood made me chairman of the Committee on Railroads, which I very much wanted, because of my desire better to understand business affairs, and also put me on the important Committee on Rules. I made progress because I studied subjects sufficiently to know a little more about them than any one else on the floor. I did not often speak but talked much with the Senators personally and came in contact with many of the business men of the state. The Boston Democrats came to be my friends and were a great help to me in later times.

My committee reported a bill transforming the Railroad Commission into a Public Service Commission, with a provision intending to define and limit the borrowing powers of railroads which we passed after a long struggle and debate. The Democratic Governor vetoed the bill, but it was passed over his veto almost unanimously. The bill came out for our trolley roads in Western Massachusetts and was adopted. He vetoed this, and his veto was overridden by a large majority. It was altogether the most enjoyable session I ever spent with any legislative body.

It had been my intention to retire at the end of my second term, but the President of the Senate was reported as being a candidate for Lieutenant-Governor, and as it seemed that I could succeed him I announced that I wished for another election. When it was too late for me to withdraw gracefully President Greenwood decided to remain in the Senate. I wanted to be President of the Senate, because it was a chance to emerge from being a purely local figure to a place of state-wide distinction and authority. I knew where the votes in the Senate lay from the hard legislative contests I had conducted, and I had them fairly well organized when I found the President was not to retire.

In this year of 1913 the division in the Republican party in Massachusetts was most pronounced. Our candidate for Governor fell to third place at the election, and another Democrat was made chief executive, carrying with him for the first time in a generation the whole state ticket. But my district returned me. When I reached my office the next morning I found President Greenwood had been defeated. Again I was ready. By three o'clock that Wednesday afternoon I was in Boston, and by Monday I had enough written pledges from the Republican Senators to insure my nomination for President of the Senate at the party caucus. It had been a real contest, but all opposition subsided and I was unanimously nominated.

The Senate showed the effects of the division in our party. It had twenty-one Republicans, seventeen Democrats and two Progressives. When the vote was cast for President on the opening day of the General Court, Senator Cox the Progressive had two votes, Senator Horgan the Democrat had seven votes, and I had thirty-one votes. I had not only become an officer of the whole Commonwealth, but I had come into possession of an influence reaching beyond the confines of my own party which I was to retain so long as I remained in public life.

Although I had arrived at the important position of President of the Massachusetts Senate in January of 1914, I had not been transported on a bed of roses. It was the result of many hard struggles in which I had made many mistakes, was to keep on making them up to the present hour, and expect to continue to make them as long as I live. We are all fallible, but experience ought to teach us not to repeat our errors.

My progress had been slow and toilsome, with little about it that was brilliant, or spectacular, the result of persistent and painstaking work, which gave it a foundation that was solid. I trust that in making this record of my own thoughts and feeling in relation to it, which necessarily bristles with the first personal pronoun, I shall not seem to be over-estimating myself, but simply relating experiences which I hope may prove to be an encouragement to others in their struggles to improve their place in the world.

It appeared to me in January, 1914, that a spirit of radicalism prevailed which unless checked was likely to prove very destructive. It had been encouraged by the opposition and by a large faction of my own party.

It consisted of the claim in general that in some way the government was to be blamed because everybody was not prosperous, because it was necessary to work for a living, and because our written constitutions, the legislatures, and the courts protected the rights of private owners especially in relation to large aggregations of property.

The previous session had been overwhelmed with a record number of bills introduced, many of them in an attempt to help the employee by impairing the property of the employer. Though anxious to improve the condition of our wage earners, I believed this doctrine would soon destroy business and deprive them of a livelihood. What was needed was a restoration of confidence in our institutions and in each other, on which economic progress might rest.

In taking the chair as President of the Senate I therefore made a short address, which I had carefully prepared, appealing to the conservative spirit of the people. I argued that the government could not relieve us from toil, that large concerns are necessary for the progress in which capital and labor all have a common interest, and I defended representative government and the integrity of the courts. The address has since been known as "Have Faith in Massachusetts." Many people in the Commonwealth had been waiting for such a word, and the effect was beyond my expectation. Confusion of thought began to disappear, and unsound legislative proposals to diminish.

The office of President of the Senate is one of great dignity and power. All the committees of the Senate are appointed by him. He has the chief place in directing legislation when the Governor is of the opposite party, as was the case in 1914. At the inauguration he presides over the joint convention of the General Court and administers the oaths of office to the Governor and Council in accordance with a formal ritual that has come from colonial days, and is much more ceremonious than the swearing-in of a President at Washington.

It did not seem to me desirable to pursue a course of partisan opposition to the Governor, and I did not do so, but rather cooperated with him in securing legislation which appeared to be for the public interest. The general lack of confidence in the country

and the depression of business caused by the reduction of the tariff rates in the fall of 1913 made it
necessary to grant large appropriations for the relief
of unemployment during the winter. But I could see
the steady decrease of the radical sentiment among
the people.

In the midst of the following summer the World
War enveloped Europe. It had a distinctly sobering
effect upon the whole people of our country. It was
very apparent in Massachusetts, where they at once
began to abandon their wanderings and seek their
old landmarks for guidance. The division in our
party was giving way to reunion. Confidence was
returning.

The Republican State Committee chose me to be
chairman of the committee on resolutions at the state
convention which met at Worcester, largely because
of the impression made by my speech at the opening
of the Senate. I drew a conservative platform, pitched
in the same key, pointing out the great mass of legislation our party had placed on the statute books for
the benefit of the wage earners and the welfare of
the people, but declaring for the strict and unim-

[109]

paired maintenance of our present social, economic and political institutions. While I did not deliver it well, in print it made an effective campaign document. After starting in the contest with little confidence, our strength increased, so that our candidate, Samuel W. McCall, received 198,627 votes and was defeated by only 11,815 plurality. All the rest of our state ticket was victorious. The political complexion of the Senate was completely changed. From a bare majority of twenty-one the Republican strength rose to thirty-three, and the opposition was reduced to seven Democrats.

My district returned me for the fourth time and I was again made President of the Senate by a unanimous vote. My opening address consisted of forty-two words, thanking the Senators for the honor and urging them in their conduct of business to be brief.

As a presiding officer it has constantly been my policy to dispatch business. It always took a long time to get all the Committees of the General Court to make their reports, but I was able to keep the daily sessions of the Senate short. I also wanted to cut down the volume of legislation. In this some

progress was made. The Blue Book of Acts and Re-
solves for 1913 had 1,763 pages, for 1914 it had
1,423, and for 1915 only 1,230, which was a very
wholesome reduction of more than thirty per cent.
People were coming to see that they must depend
on themselves rather than on legislation for success.

Massachusetts was beginning to suffer from a
great complication of laws and restrictive regulations, from a multiplicity of Boards and Commissions, which had reached about one hundred, and
from a large increase in the number of people on
the public pay rolls, all of which was necessarily accompanied with a much larger cost of state government that had to be met by collecting more revenue
from the taxpayers. The people began to realize that
something was wrong and began to wonder whether
more laws, more regulations, and more taxes, were
really any benefit to them. They were becoming tired
of agitation, criticism and destructive policies and
wished to return to constructive methods.

When I went home at the end of the 1915 session
it was with the intention of remaining in private life
and giving all my attention to the law. During the

winter the Lieutenant-Governor had announced that he would seek the nomination for Governor which caused some mention of me as his successor, but I was President of the Senate and did not propose to impair my usefulness in that position by involving it in an effort to secure some other office, so I gave the matter no attention. A very estimable man who had done much party service and was a brilliant platform speaker had already become a candidate, but although my record in the General Court was that of a liberal, the business interests turned to me. In this they were not alone as the event disclosed. To the people I seemed, in some way that I cannot explain, to represent confidence. When the situation became apparent to me I went to Boston and made the simple statement in the press that I was a candidate for Lieutenant-Governor, without any reasons or any elaboration.

It was at this time that my intimate acquaintance began with Mr. Frank W. Stearns. I had met him in a casual way for a year or two but only occasionally. In the spring he had suggested that he would like to support me for Lieutenant-Governor. He was a merchant of high character and very much respected by all who knew him, but entirely without experience in politics. He came as an entirely fresh force in public affairs, unhampered by any of the animosities that usually attach to a veteran politician. It was a great compliment to me to attract the interest of such a man, and his influence later became of large value to the party in the Commonwealth and nation. I always felt considerable pride of accomplishment in getting the active support of men like him. While Mr. Stearns always overestimated me, he nevertheless was a great help to me. He never obtruded or sought any favor for himself or any other person, but his whole effort was always disinterested and entirely devoted to assisting me when I indicated I wished him to do so. It is doubtful if any other public man ever had so valuable and unselfish a friend.

My activities were such that I began to see more of the Honorable W. Murray Crane. When he came to Boston he was accustomed to have me at breakfast in his rooms at the hotel. Although he had large interests about which there was constant legislation he never mentioned the subject to me or made any suggestion about any of my official actions. Had I sought his advice he would have told me to consult my own judgment and vote for what the public interest required, without any thought of him. He confirmed my opinion as to the value of a silence which avoids creating a situation where one would otherwise not exist, and the bad taste and the danger of arousing animosities and advertising an opponent by making any attack on him. In all political affairs he had a wonderful wisdom, and in everything he was preeminently a man of judgment, who was the most disinterested public servant I ever saw and the greatest influence for good government with which I ever came in contact. What would I not have given to have had him by my side when I was President! His end came just before the election of 1920.

These men were additional examples of good influences coming into my life, to which I referred in relating the experience of some of my younger days. I cannot see that I sought them but they came. Perhaps it was because I was ready to receive them.

In the summer of 1915 politics became very active in Massachusetts. There was a sharp campaign for the nomination for Governor, my own effort to secure the Lieutenant-Governorship, and many minor contests. I shall always remember that Augustus P. Gardner, then in Congress, honored me by becoming one of the committee of five who conducted my campaign. Many local meetings were held, calling for much speaking. In the end Samuel W. McCall was renominated for Governor. I was named as candidate for Lieutenant-Governor by a vote of about 75,000 to 50,000. The news reached my father on the one-hundredth anniversary of the birth of his father. My campaign was carried on in careful compliance with the law, and the expense was within the allowed limit of $1,500, which was contributed by numerous people. I was thus under no especial obligation to any one for raising money for me.

In the campaign for election I toured the state with Mr. McCall, making open-air speeches from automobiles during the day, and finishing with an indoor rally in the evening. It was the hardest kind of work but most fascinating. I remember that Warren G. Harding and Nicholas Longworth came into the state to promote our election and spoke with us at a large meeting one night at Lowell.

I did not refer to my own candidacy, but spent all my time advocating the election of Mr. McCall. He was a character that fitted into the situation most admirably. He was liberal without being visionary and conservative without being reactionary. The twenty-five years he had spent in public life gave him a remarkable equipment for discussing the issues of a campaign. Whatever information was needed concerning the state government I was in a position to supply. Much emphasis was placed by me on the urgent necessity of preventing further increases in state and national expense and of a drastic reduction wherever possible. The state was ready for that kind of a message.

When the election of 1915 came, Mr. McCall won by 6,313 votes and my plurality was 52,204. After having been held five years by Democrats, the Governorship of Massachusetts was restored to the Republican party, where it was to remain for the next fifteen years and probably much longer. The extended struggle in which the Republicans had been engaged to restore the people of Massachusetts to their allegiance to sound government under a re-united party had at last been successful. With that prolonged effort I had been intimately associated.

The office of Lieutenant-Governor of Massachu-setts differs from that of most states. As already dis-closed he does not preside over the Senate. The con-stitution of our Commonwealth is older than the Federal Constitution and so followed the old colo-nial system, while most of the states have followed the Federal system. I was *ex officio* a member of the Governor's Council and chairman of the Finance and Pardon committees. As the Council met but one day each week I was pleased with the renewed opportunity I expected to have to practice law. But it soon developed that I must be away so much that I asked Ralph W. Hemenway to become associated with me, and he has since carried on my law office so successfully that it has become his law office rather than mine.

It has become the custom in our country to expect all Chief Executives, from the President down, to conduct activities analogous to an entertainment bureau. No occasion is too trivial for its promoters to invite them to attend and deliver an address. It appeared to be the practice of Governor McCall to accept all these invitations and when the time came, to attend what he could of them, and parcel the rest out among his subordinates. In this way I became very much engaged. It was an honor to represent the Governor, and a part of my duties according to our practice. Some days I went to several meetings for that purpose, ranging well into the night, so I was obliged to stay in Boston most of the time.

It was during this period that I wrote nearly all of the speeches afterwards published in "Have Faith in Massachusetts." They were short and mostly committed to memory for delivery. This forced me to be a constant student of public questions.

It did not seem best for me to take a very active part in the Presidential primaries of 1916, but I quietly supported the regular ticket for delegates, which was elected. We had at least three candidates for President in Massachusetts, with all of whom I was on friendly terms, as I had never allied myself with any faction of the party, but I felt the convention did the wise thing in turning to the great statesman Charles Evans Hughes, and I supported him actively in the campaign for election. He carried Massachusetts by a small vote. My renomination came without opposition, as did that of the Governor, who had a plurality of 46,240 at the election. My own was 84,930.

During the summer I had been chairman of a special commission to consider the financial condition of the Boston Elevated Street Railway, and helped make a report recommending that the Governor be authorized to appoint a Board of Trustees who should have the control of this property and be vested with authority to fix a rate of fare sufficient to pay the costs of operation and a fair return to the stockholders. This was adopted by the General Court and solved the pressing problem of street railway transportation, which became so acute on account of the increasing costs of operation. Later the plan was applied to the other large company in the eastern part of the state. It was not perfect, but saved the properties from destruction and gave a fair means of travel at cost, which was to be ascertained by public authority.

It was in the ensuing year that the United States entered the World War. While this took most of our thoughts off local affairs it did not prevent opposition to the renomination of Governor McCall. Had it been successful it would have deferred any chance for me to run for Governor for two or three years and probably indefinitely. Under the circumstances most of my friends supported the Governor, and he was renominated by a wide margin. I had no opposition. But interest in the election was not great, so that the vote was light. Nevertheless the Governor ran 90,479 votes ahead of his nearest competitor. In my own contest my opponent secured the Democratic, the Progressive and the Prohibition nomination. I did not think the combination would prove helpful to him, and it did not. He fell off 77,000 from the vote of his predecessor, and I won by 101,731.

While the United States had been engaged in the World War every public man, and I among them, had been constantly employed in its many activities. It increased every function of government from the administration in Washington down to the smallest town office. The whole nation seemed to be endowed with a new spirit, unified and solidified and willing to make any sacrifice for the cause of liberty. I was constantly before public gatherings explaining the needs of the time for men, money and supplies. Sometimes I was urging subscriptions for war loans, sometimes contributions to the great charities, or again speaking to the workmen engaged in construction or the manufacture of munitions. The response which the people made and the organizing power of the country were all manifestations that it was wonderful to contemplate. The entire nation awoke to a new life.

It was no secret that I desired to be Governor. Under the custom of promotion in Massachusetts a man who did not expect to be advanced would scarcely be willing to be Lieutenant-Governor. But I did nothing in the way of organizing my friends to secure the nomination. It is much better not to press a candidacy too much, but to let it develop on its own merits without artificial stimulation. If the people want a man they will nominate him, if they do not want him he had best let the nomination go to another.

The Governor very much desired to be United States Senator, but made no statement indicating he would seek that honor which would cause him to retire from his present office. Neither I nor my friends approached him or sought to influence him. Finally he called me aside and told me to announce that I would run for Governor, which I did. As no one knew what he had told me, some supposed I would run against him, which I would not have done.

I had a strong liking for this veteran public servant, and so I felt sure he liked me. He was away on many occasions, which under the constitution left me as Acting Governor, but at such times I was always careful not to encroach upon his domain. While I may have differed with my subordinates I have always supported loyally my superiors. They have never found me organizing a camp in opposition to them. Finally the Governor sought the Senatorship, but before his campaign was under way he very manfully announced that as the country was at war he was entirely unwilling to divert public attention from the national defense to promote his political fortune and therefore withdrew. My nomination was again unanimous.

The campaign was difficult. The really great qualities of my principal colleague, Senator John W. Weeks, had been displayed mostly in Washington and were not appreciated by his home people. A violent epidemic of influenza prevented us from having a State Convention, or holding the usual meetings, and the party organization was not very effective. In spite of my protest and the fact that we were engaged in a tremendous war, criticism was too often made of President Wilson and his administration. My own efforts were spent in urging that the people and government of Massachusetts should all join in their support of the national government in prosecuting the war. While I was elected by only 16,773, Senator Weeks to my lasting regret was defeated, so the state and nation lost for a time the benefit of his valuable public service. Later he was in the Cabinet where he remained until, during my term, he retired due to ill health, and did not long survive.

Again I supposed I had reached the summit of any possible political preferment and was quite content to finish my public career as Governor of Massachusetts—an office that has always been held in the highest honor by the people of the Commonwealth.

To get a few days' rest I went to Maine the next Friday after the election. It was there that I was awakened in the middle of Sunday night to be told that the Armistice had been signed. I returned to Boston the following day to take part in the celebration. What the end of the four years of carnage meant those who remember it will never forget and those who do not can never be told. The universal joy, the enormous relief, found expression from all the people in a spontaneous outburst of thanksgiving.

While the war was done, its problems were to confront the state and nation for many years. I was to meet them as Governor and President. They will remain with us for two generations. Such is the curse of war.

In my inaugural address I dwelt on the need of promoting the public health, education, and the opportunity for employment at fair wages in accordance with the right of the people to be well born, well reared, well educated, well employed and well paid. I also stressed the necessity of keeping government expenses as low as possible, assisting in every possible way the reestablishing of the returning veterans, and reorganizing the numerous departments in accordance with a recent change of the constitution which limited their number to twenty.

There being no Executive Mansion the Governor has no especial social duties, so I kept my quarters at the Adams House, as I had always lived there when in Boston, where Mrs. Coolidge came sometimes; but as our boys needed her she staid for the most part in Northampton. She never had taken any part in my political life, but had given her attention to our home. It was not until we went to Washington that she came into public prominence and favor.

[125]

In February, President Wilson landed at Boston on his return from France and spoke at a large meeting, where I made a short address of welcome, pledging him my support in helping settle the remaining war problems. I then began a friendly personal relation with him and Mrs. Wilson which has always continued. Our service men were constantly returning and had to be aided in getting back into private employment. About $20,000,000 was paid them out of the state treasury.

In the confusion attending the end of the war the work of legislation dragged on well into the summer. While I did not veto many of the bills which were passed, I did reject a measure to increase the salaries of members of the General Court from $1,000 to $1,500, but my objection was not sustained.

In the great upward movement of wages that had taken place those paid by street railways had not been proportionately increased. It is very difficult to raise fares, so sufficient money for this purpose had not been available, though some advances had been made. Because of this situation a strike oc-

curred in midsummer on the Boston Elevated that
tied up nearly all the street transportation in the city
district for three or four days. Finally I helped negotiate an agreement to send the matter to arbitration, so that work was resumed. The men secured a
very material raise in wages, which I feel later conditions fully justified.

In August I went to Vermont. On my return I
found that difficulties in the Police Department of
Boston were growing serious and made a statement
to the reporters at the State House that I should support Commissioner Edwin U. Curtis in his decisions
concerning their adjustment. I felt he was entitled
to every confidence.

The trouble arose over the proposal of the policemen, who had long been permitted to maintain a
local organization of their own, to form a union and
affiliate with the American Federation of Labor.
That was contrary to a long-established rule of the
Department, which was agreed to by each member
when he went on the force and had the effect of law.

When the policemen's union persisted in its course
I was urged by a committee appointed by the Mayor

to interfere and attempt to make Commissioner Curtis settle the dispute by arbitration. The Governor appoints the Commissioner and probably could remove him, but he has no more jurisdiction over his acts than he has over the Judges of the Courts; besides, I did not see how it was possible to arbitrate the question of the authority of the law, or of the necessity of obedience to the rules of the Department and the orders of the Commissioner. These principles were the heart of the whole controversy and the only important questions at issue. It can readily be seen how important they were and what the effect might have been if they had not been maintained. I decided to support them whatever the consequences might be. I fully expected it would result in my defeat in the coming campaign for reelection as Governor.

While I had no direct responsibility for the conduct of police matters in Boston, yet as the Chief Executive it was my general duty to require the laws to be enforced, so I remained in Boston and kept carefully informed of conditions. I knew I might be called on to act at any time.

On Sunday, September seventh, I went to Northampton by motor and remained overnight as I had
an engagement to speak before a state convention of
the American Federation of Labor at Greenfield
Monday morning, which I fulfilled. I left that town
at once for Boston, stopping at Fitchburg to call my
office to learn if there were any new developments.
I reached Boston after four o'clock that afternoon,
and had a conference with some of the representatives of the city. I did not leave Boston again for a
long time.

When it became perfectly apparent that the policemen's union was acting in violation of the rules
of the Department the leaders were brought before
the Commissioner on charges, tried and removed
from office, whereat about three-quarters of the
force left the Department in a body at about five
o'clock on the afternoon of Tuesday, September
ninth. This number was much larger than had been
expected.

The Metropolitan Police of more than one hundred, and the State Police of thirty or forty men,
had been kept in readiness and were at once put on

duty, the Motor Corps of the State Guard was held at the armory, and that night I kept the Attorney General, the Adjutant General and my Secretary at my hotel to be ready to respond to any call for help. As everything was quiet the Motor Corps went home. Around midnight bands of men appeared on the street, who broke many shop windows and carried away quantities of the goods which were on display. Many arrests were made, but the remaining police and their reinforcements were not sufficient to prevent the disorder. I knew nothing of this until morning.

The disorder of Tuesday night was most reprehensible, but it was only an incident. It had little relation to the real issues. I have always felt that I should have called out the State Guard as soon as the police left their posts. The Commissioner did not feel this was necessary. The Mayor, who was a man of high character, and a personal friend, but of the opposite party, had conferred with me. He had the same authority as the Governor to call out all the Guard in the City of Boston. It would be very unusual for a Governor to act except on the request of the local authorities. No disorder existed, and it would have been rather a violent assumption that it was threatened, but it could have been made. Such action probably would have saved some property, but would have decided no issue. In fact it would have made it more difficult to maintain the position Mr. Curtis had taken, and which I was supporting, because the issue was not understood, and the disorder focused public attention on it, and showed just what it meant to have a police force that did not obey orders.

On reaching my office in the morning it was reported to me that the Mayor was calling out the State Guard of Boston to report about five o'clock that afternoon. He also requested me to furnish more troops. I supplemented his action by calling substantially the entire State Guard to report at once. They gathered at their armories and were patrolling the streets in a few hours. When they came with their muskets in their hands with bayonets fixed there was little more trouble from disorder.

It was soon reported to me that the Mayor, acting under a special law, had taken charge of the police force of the city, and by putting a Guard officer in command had virtually displaced the Commissioner, who came to me in great distress. If he was to be superseded I thought the men that he had discharged might be taken back and the cause lost. Certainly they and the rest of the policemen's union must have rejoiced at his discomfort. Thinking I knew what to do, I consulted the law as is my custom. I found a general statute that gives the Governor authority to call on any police officer in the state to assist him. I showed this to the Attorney General and to Ex-Attorney General Herbert Parker, who was advising Mr. Curtis. They thought I was right and consulted a profound judge of law, Ex-Attorney General Albert E. Pillsbury, who confirmed their opinions. The strike occurred Tuesday night, the Guard were called Wednesday, and Thursday I issued a General Order restoring Mr. Curtis to his place as Commissioner in control of the police, and made a proclamation calling on all citizens to assist me in preserving order, and especially directing all police officers in Boston to obey the orders of Mr. Curtis.

This was the important contribution I made to

the tactics of the situation, which has never been fully realized. To Mr. Curtis should go the credit for raising the issue and enforcing the principle that police should not affiliate with any outside body, whether of wage earners or of wage payers, but should remain unattached, impartial officers of the law, with sole allegiance to the public. In this I supported him.

When rumors started of a strike at the power house which furnished electricity for all Boston, a naval vessel was run up to the station with plenty of electricians on board ready to go over the side and keep the plant in operation. A wagon train of supplies, arms, and ammunition was brought in from Camp Devens and all the State Guard mobilized. A statement was made by President Wilson strongly condemning the defection of the police. Volunteer police began to come in, and over half a million dollars was raised by popular subscription to meet necessary expenses in caring for dependents of the Guard and even for helping the families of some of the police who left their posts. Later I helped these men in securing other employment, but refused to allow

[133]

them again to be policemen. Public feeling became very much aroused. While offers of support came from every quarter the opposition was very active.

Soon, Samuel Gompers began to telegraph me asking the removal of Mr. Curtis and the reinstatement of the union policemen. This required me to make a reply in which I stated among other things that "There is no right to strike against the public safety by any body, any time, any where." This phrase caught the attention of the nation. It was beginning to be clear that if voluntary associations were to be permitted to substitute their will for the authority of public officials the end of our government was at hand. The issue was nothing less than whether the law which the people had made through their duly authorized agencies should be supreme.

This issue I took to the people in my campaign for reelection as Governor. Though I was hampered by an attack of influenza and spoke but three or four times, I was able to make the issue plain even beyond the confines of Massachusetts. Many of the wage earners both organized and unorganized, who knew I had always treated them fairly, must have supported me, for I won by 125,101 votes. The people decided in favor of the integrity of their own government. President Wilson sent me a telegram of congratulations.

I felt at the time that the speeches I made and the statements I issued had a clearness of thought and revealed a power I had not before been able to express, which confirmed my belief that, when a duty comes to us, with it a power comes to enable us to perform it. I was not thinking so much of the Governorship, which I already had, as of the grave danger to the country if the voters did not decide correctly. My faith that the people would respond to the truth was justified.

The requirements of the situation as it developed seem clear and plain now, and easy to decide, but as they arose they were very complicated and involved in many immaterial issues. The right thing to do never requires any subterfuges, it is always simple and direct. That is the reason that intrigue usually falls of its own weight.

After the election I had the work of making the appointments in order to reduce the entire state ad-

[135]

ministration to the limit of twenty Departments and
a special session of the General Court to deal with
some street railway problems, so I had little time to
think of politics. But I soon learned that many people in the country were thinking of me.

The two years that I served as Governor were a
time of transition from war to peace. New problems
constantly arose, great confusion prevailed, nothing
was settled and it was possible only to feel my way
from day to day. But they were years of progress if
partly in a negative way. The new position of the
wage earners was perfected and solidified. A forty-
eight-hour week for women and minors was established by a bill passed by the General Court, which
I signed. The budget system went fully into effect
the first year I was Governor and helped keep the
state finances in good condition. The departments
were reorganized, and the street railways given relief. In my second year a bill was passed allowing
the sale of beer with a 2.75 per cent alcoholic content, which I vetoed because I thought it was in violation of the Constitution which I had sworn to de-
fend. The veto was sustained. A constant struggle

CALVIN COOLIDGE
At Amherst College

was going on to keep the costs of living down and the rate of wages up. A State Commission was held in office with increased powers to resist profiteering in the necessaries of life. In the depression of 1920 some of our banks and manufacturers found themselves in difficulties. All of these things reached the Governor in one form or another. But, in general, conditions were such that the entire efforts of the people were engaged in easing themselves down. There was little opportunity to direct their attention towards constructive action. They were clearing away the refuse from the great conflagration preparatory to rebuilding on a grander and more pretentious scale. Nothing was natural, everything was artificial. So much energy had to be expended in keeping the ship of state on a straight course that there was little left to carry it ahead. But when I finished my two terms in January, 1921, the demobilization of the country was practically complete, people had found themselves again, and were ready to undertake the great work of reconstruction in which they have since been so successfully engaged. In that work we have seen the people of America

[137]

create a new heaven and a new earth. The old things have passed away, giving place to a glory never before experienced by any people of our world.

IN NATIONAL POLITICS

CHAPTER FOUR

IN NATIONAL POLITICS

N O doubt it was the police strike of Boston that brought me into national prominence. That furnished the occasion and I took advantage of the opportunity. I was ready to meet the emergency. Just what lay behind that event I was never able to learn. Sometimes I have mistrusted that it was a design to injure me politically; if so it was only to recoil upon the perpetrators, for it increased my political power many fold. Still there was a day or two when the event hung in the balance, when the Police Commissioner of Boston, Edwin U. Curtis, was apparently cast aside discredited, and my efforts to give him any support indicated my own undoing. But I soon had him reinstated, and there was a strong expression of public opinion in our favor.

The year 1919 had not produced much on the
[141]

positive side of our political life. President Wilson had returned from the peace conference at Paris determined to have the United States join the League of Nations as established in the final Treaty of Versailles. He found opposition in the Senate both within and without his own party. In attempting to gain the approval of the country he had made his trip across the continent and returned a broken man never to regain his strength. For eight years he had so dominated his party that it had not produced any one else with a marked ability for leadership. During these months the contest was raging in the Senate over the peace treaty, but as a result it had put the leadership of our party in a negative position, which never appeals to the popular imagination, and besides in the country many Republicans favored a ratification of the treaty with adequate reservations. Many of the Senators on our side cast their vote for that proposal, which would have prevailed but for the opposition of the regular administration Democrats. In this confusion no dominant popular figure emerged in the Congress, but many ambitions became apparent.

Following my decisive victory in November there very soon came to be mention of me as a Presidential candidate. About Thanksgiving time Senator Lodge came to me and voluntarily requested that he should present my name to the national Republican convention. He wished to go as a delegate with that understanding. Of course I told him I could not make any decision in relation to being a candidate, but I would try to arrange matters so that he could be a delegate at large. When he left for Washington he gave out an interview saying that Massachusetts should support me.

Very soon a movement of considerable dimensions started both in my home state and in other sections of the country to secure delegates who would support me. An old friend and long time Secretary of the Republican National Committee, James B. Reynolds, was placed in charge of the movement, and I was gaining considerable strength. Senator Crane in his own quiet but highly efficient way became very interested and let it be known that I had his support, as did Speaker Gillett, who is now our Senator, but then represented my home district in Congress. They both went as delegates pledged to me.

Already several candidates were making a very active campaign. The two most conspicuous were Major General Leonard Wood and Governor Frank O. Lowden. Senator Hiram Johnson had considerable support, and in a more modest way Senator Warren G. Harding was in the field. In addition to these, several of the states had favorite sons. It soon began to be reported that very large sums of money were being used in the primaries.

When I came to give the matter serious attention, and comprehended more fully what would be involved in a contest of this kind, I realized that I was not in a position to become engaged in it. I was Governor of Massachusetts, and my first duty was to that office. It would not be possible for me, with the legislature in session, to be going about the country actively participating in an effort to secure delegates, and I was totally unwilling to have a large sum of money raised and spent in my behalf.

I soon became convinced also that I was in danger of creating a situation in which some people in

Massachusetts could permit it to be reported in the press that they were for me when they were not at heart for me and would give me little support in the convention. It would, however, prevent their having to make a public choice as between other candidates and would help them in getting elected as delegates. There was nothing unusual in this situation. It was simply a condition that always has to be met in politics. Of course the strategy of the other candidates was to prevent me from having a solid Massachusetts delegation. Moreover, I did not wish to use the office of Governor in an attempt to prosecute a campaign for nomination for some other office. I therefore made a public statement announcing that I was unwilling to appear as a candidate and would not enter my name in any contest at the primaries. This left me in a position where I ran no risk of embarrassing the great office of Governor of Massachusetts. That was my answer to the situation.

Nevertheless a considerable activity was kept up in my behalf, and some money expended, mostly in circulating a book of my speeches. In the Massachusetts primaries six or seven delegates were chosen who were for General Wood, and while the rest were nominally for me several of them were really more favorable to some other candidate, partly because they supposed a Massachusetts man could never be nominated, and if the choice was going outside the state, they had strong preferences as between the other possibilities.

At a state convention in South Dakota held very early to express a preference for national candidates I had been declared their choice for Vice-President. Some people in Oregon desired to accord me a like honor. As I did not wish my name to appear in any contest and did not care to be Vice-President I declined to be considered for that office. In my native state of Vermont it was proposed to enter my name in the primary as candidate for President, which I could not permit. Nevertheless it was written on the ballot by many of the voters at the polls.

When the Republican National Convention met at Chicago, Senator Lodge, who was elected its chairman, had indicated that he did not wish to present my name, so it was arranged that Speaker Gillett should make the nominating speech. Massachusetts had thirty-five delegates. On the first ballot I received twenty-eight of their votes and six others from scattering states, making my total thirty-four. As the balloting proceeded a considerable number of the Massachusetts delegates, feeling I had no chance, voted for other candidates, but a majority remained with me until the final ballot when all but one went elsewhere, and Senator Warren G. Harding was nominated. My friends in the convention did all they could for me, and several states were at times ready to come to me if the entire Massachusetts delegation would lead the way, but some of them refused to vote for me, so the support of other states could not be secured.

While I do not think it was so intended I have always been of the opinion that this turned out to be much the best for me. I had no national experience. What I have ever been able to do has been the result of first learning how to do it. I am not gifted with intuition. I need not only hard work but experience to be ready to solve problems. The Presidents who have gone to Washington without first having held some national office have been at great disadvantage.

It takes them a long time to become acquainted with the Federal officeholders and the Federal Government. Meanwhile they have had difficulty in dealing with the situation.

The convention of 1920 was largely under the domination of a coterie of United States Senators. They maneuvered it into adopting a platform and nominating a President in ways that were not satisfactory to a majority of the delegates. When the same forces undertook for a third time to dictate the action of the convention in naming a Vice-President, the delegates broke away from them and literally stampeded to me.

Massachusetts did not present my name, because my friends knew I did not wish to be Vice-President, but Judge Wallace McCamant of Oregon placed me in nomination and was quickly seconded by North Dakota and some other states. I received about three-quarters of all the votes cast. When this honor came to me I was pleased to accept, and it was especially agreeable to be associated with Senator Harding, whom I knew well and liked.

When our campaign opened, the situation was

complex. Many Republicans did not like the somewhat uncertain tone of the platform concerning the
League of Nations. Though it was generally con-
ceded that the bitter-enders had dictated the platform there were some who felt it was not explicit
enough in denouncing the League with all its works
and everything foreign, and a much larger body of
Republicans were much disappointed that it did not
declare in favor of ratifying the treaty with reservations.

The Massachusetts Republican State Convention
in the fall of 1919 had adopted a plank favoring immediate ratification with suitable reservations which
would safeguard American interests. While later
the treaty had been rejected by the Senate it was still
necessary to make a formal agreement of peace with
the Central Powers, and for that purpose some treaty
would be necessary. Many Republicans favored our
entry into the League as a method of closing up the
war period and helping stabilize world conditions.
Senator Crane had taken that position in Massachusetts and repeated it again at Chicago.

Since that time the situation has changed. The

war period has closed and a separate treaty has been made and ratified. The more I have seen of the conduct of our foreign relations the more I am convinced that we are better off out of the League. Our government is not organized in a way that would enable us adequately to deal with it. Nominally our foreign affairs are in the hands of the President. Actually the Senate is always attempting to interfere, too often in a partisan way and many times in opposition to the President. Our country is not racially homogeneous. While the several nationalities represented here are loyal to the United States, yet when differences arise between European countries, each group is naturally in sympathy with the nation of its origin. Our actions in the League would constantly be embarrassed by this situation at home. The votes of our delegates there would all the time disturb our domestic tranquillity here. We have come to realize this situation very completely now, but in 1920 it was not so clear.

At that time we were close to the war. Our sympathies were very much with our allies and a great body of sentiment in our country, which may be called the missionary spirit, was strongly in favor of helping Europe. To them the League meant an instrument for that end. That was a praiseworthy spirit and had to be reckoned with in dealing with the people in a political campaign. This sentiment was very marked in the East where it had a strong hold on a very substantial element of the Republican party.

While I was taking a short vacation in Vermont several thousand people came to my father's home to greet me. I spent most of my time, however, in preparing my speech of acceptance. The notification ceremonies were held on a pleasant afternoon in midsummer at Northampton in Allen Field, which was part of the college grounds, and its former President, the venerable Dr. L. Clark Seelye, presided. The chairman of the notification committee was Governor Morrow of Kentucky. A great throng representing many different states was in attendance to hear my address. I was careful to reassure those who feared we were not proposing to continue our cooperation with Europe in attempting to solve the war problems in a way that would provide for a permanent peace of the world.

Not being the head of the ticket, of course, it was not my place to raise issues or create policies, but I had the privilege of discussing those already declared in the platform or stated in the addresses of Senator Harding. This I undertook to do in a speech I made at Portland, Maine, where I again pointed out the wish of our party to have our country associated with other countries in advancing human welfare. Later in the campaign I reiterated this position at New York.

This was not intended as a subterfuge to win votes, but as a candid statement of party principles. It was later to be put into practical effect by President Harding, in the important treaty dealing with our international relations in the Pacific Ocean, in the agreement for the limitation of naval armaments, in the proposal to enter the World Court, and finally by me in the World Peace Treaty. All that I said and more in justification of support of the Republican ticket by those interested in promoting peace, without committing our country to interfere where we had little interest, has been abundantly borne out by the events.

Shortly before election I made a tour of eight days,

going from Philadelphia by special train west to Tennessee and Kentucky and south as far as North Carolina. We had a most encouraging reception on this trip, speaking out-of-doors, mostly from the rear platform during the day, with an indoor meeting at night. During the campaign I spoke in about a dozen states.

The country was already feeling acutely the results of deflation. Business was depressed. For months following the Armistice we had persisted in a course of much extravagance and reckless buying. Wages had been paid that were not earned. The whole country, from the national government down, had been living on borrowed money. Pay day had come, and it was found our capital had been much impaired. In an address at Philadelphia I contended that the only sure method of relieving this distress was for the country to follow the advice of Benjamin Franklin and begin to work and save. Our productive capacity is sufficient to maintain us all in a state of prosperity if we give sufficient attention to thrift and industry. Within a year the country had adopted that course, which has brought an era of great plenty.

When the election came it appeared that we had held practically the entire Republican vote and had gained enormously from all those groups who have been in this country so short a time that they still retain a marked race consciousness. Many of them had left Europe to escape from the prevailing conditions there. While they were loyal to the United States they did not wish to become involved in any old world disputes, were greatly relieved that the war was finished, and generally opposed to the League of Nations. Such a combination gave us an overwhelming victory.

After election it was necessary for me to attend a good many celebrations. My home town of Northampton had a large mass meeting at which several speeches were made. In Boston a series of dinners and lunches were given in my honor. Shortly before Christmas Mrs. Coolidge and I paid a brief visit to Mr. and Mrs. Harding at their home in Marion, Ohio. They received us in the most gracious manner. It was no secret to us why their friends had so much affection for them.

We discussed at length the plans for his administration. The members of his Cabinet were considered and he renewed the invitation to me, already publicly expressed, to sit with them. The policies he wished to adopt for restoring the prosperity of the country by reducing taxes and revising the tariff were referred to more casually. He was sincerely devoted to the public welfare and desirous of improving the condition of the people.

When at last another Governor was inaugurated to take my place and the guns on Boston Common were giving him their first salute, Mrs. Coolidge and I were leaving for home from the North Station on the afternoon train which I had used so much before I was Governor. It had only day coaches and no parlor car, but we were accustomed to travel that way and only anxious to go home. For nine years I had been in public life in Boston.

During the winter I made an address before the Vermont Historical Society at Montpelier and spoke later at the Town Hall in New York for a group of ladies who were restoring the birthplace of Theodore Roosevelt.

After a brief stay at Northampton, Mrs. Coolidge and I went to Atlanta where I spoke before the Southern Tariff Association. A great deal of hospitality was lavished upon us by the state officials and the people in the city. In a few days we went to Asheville, North Carolina, where we remained about two weeks. The Grove Park Inn entertained us with everything that could be wished, and the region was delightful.

When the Massachusetts electors met, Judge Henry P. Field of the firm where I read law, who had moved my admission to the Bar, now had the experience of nominating me for Vice-President. Twenty-four years had intervened between these two services which he performed for me.

The time soon came for us to go to Washington. A large crowd of our friends was at the station to bid us goodbye although the hour was very early. We went a few days before March 4 in order to have a little time to get settled. The Vice-President and Mrs. Marshall met us and gave us every attention and courtesy. When Mr. and Mrs. Harding arrived, we went to the station to meet them and they took us back with them to the New Willard—where we too were staying—in the White House car President Wilson sent for them.

About ten-thirty the next morning a committee of the Congress came to escort us to the White House where the President and Mrs. Wilson joined us and we went to the Capitol. Soon President Wilson sent for me and said his health was such it would not be wise for him to remain for the inauguration and bade me goodbye. I never saw him again except at a distance, but he sent me a most sympathetic letter when I became President. Such was the passing of a great world figure.

As I had already taken a leading part in seven inaugurations and witnessed four others in Massachusetts, the experience was not new to me, but I was struck by the lack of order and formality that prevailed. A part of the ceremony takes place in the Senate Chamber and a part on the east portico, which destroys all semblance of unity and continuity. I was sworn in before the Senate and made a very brief address dwelling on the great value of a deliberative body as a safeguard of our liberties.

[157]

It was a clear but crisp spring day out-of-doors where the oath was administered to the President by Chief Justice White. The inaugural address was able and well received. President Harding had an impressive delivery, which never failed to interest and hold his audience. I was to hear him many times in the next two years, but whether on formal occasions or in the freedom of Gridiron dinners, his charm and effectiveness never failed.

When the inauguration was over I realized that the same thing for which I had worked in Massachusetts had been accomplished in the nation. The radicalism which had tinged our whole political and economic life from soon after 1900 to the World War period was passed. There were still echoes of it, and some of its votaries remained, but its power was gone. The country had little interest in mere destructive criticism. It wanted the progress that alone comes from constructive policies.

It had been our intention to take a house in Washington, but we found none to our liking. They were too small or too large. It was necessary for me to live within my income, which was little more than my salary and was charged with the cost of sending my boys to school. We therefore took two bedrooms with a dining room, and large reception room at the New Willard where we had every convenience.

It is difficult to conceive a person finding himself in a situation which calls on him to maintain a position he cannot pay for. Any other course for me would have been cut short by the barnyard philosophy of my father, who would have contemptuously referred to such action as the senseless imitation of a fowl which was attempting to light higher than it could roost. There is no dignity quite so impressive, and no independence quite so important, as living within your means. In our country a small income is usually less embarrassing than the possession of a large one.

But my experience has convinced me that an official residence with suitable maintenance should be provided for the Vice-President. Under the present system he is not lacking in dignity but he has no fixed position. The great office should have a settled and permanent habitation and a place, irrespective of the financial ability of its temporary occupant.

While I was glad to be relieved of the responsibility of a public establishment, nevertheless, it is a duty the second officer of the nation should assume. It would be much more in harmony with our theory of equality if each Vice-President held the same position in the Capital City.

Very much is said and written concerning the amount of dining out that the Vice-President does. As the President is not available for social dinners of course the next officer in rank is much sought after for such occasions. But like everything else that is sent out of Washington for public consumption the reports are exaggerated. Probably the average of these dinners during the season does not exceed three a week, and as the Senate is in session after twelve o'clock each week day, there is no opportunity for lunches or teas.

When we first went to Washington Mrs. Coolidge and I quite enjoyed the social dinners. As we were always the ranking guests we had the privilege of arriving last and leaving first, so that we were usually home by ten o'clock. It will be seen that this was far from burdensome. We found it a most en-

[160]

joyable opportunity for getting acquainted and could scarcely comprehend how anyone who had the privilege of sitting at a table surrounded by representatives of the Cabinet, the Congress, the Diplomatic Corps and the Army and Navy would not find it interesting.

Presiding over the Senate was fascinating to me. That branch of the Congress has its own methods and traditions which may strike the outsider as peculiar, but more familiarity with them would disclose that they are only what long experience has demonstrated to be the best methods of conducting its business. It may seem that debate is endless, but there is scarcely a time when it is not informing, and, after all, the power to compel due consideration is the distinguishing mark of a deliberative body. If the Senate is anything it is a great deliberative body and if it is to remain a safeguard of liberty it must remain a deliberative body. I was entertained and instructed by the debates. However it may appear in the country, no one can become familiar with the inside workings of the Senate without gaining a great respect for it. The country is safe in its hands.

[161]

At first I intended to become a student of the Senate rules and I did learn much about them, but I soon found that the Senate had but one fixed rule, subject to exceptions of course, which was to the effect that the Senate would do anything it wanted to do whenever it wanted to do it. When I had learned that, I did not waste much time on the other rules, because they were so seldom applied. The assistant to the Secretary of the Senate could be relied on to keep me informed on other parliamentary questions. But the President of the Senate can and does exercise a good deal of influence over its deliberations. The Constitution gives him the power to preside, which is the power to recognize whom he will. That often means that he decides what business is to be taken up and who is to have the floor for debate at any specific time.

Nor is the impression that it is a dilatory body never arriving at decisions correct. In addition to acting on the thousands of nominations, and the numerous treaties, it passes much more legislation than the House. But it is true that unanimous consent is often required to close debate, and because of the great power each Senator is therefore permitted to exercise—which is often a veto power, making one Senator a majority of the ninety-six Senators—great care should be exercised by the states in their choice of Senators. Nothing is more dangerous to good government than great power in improper hands. If the Senate has any weakness it is because the people have sent to that body men lacking the necessary ability and character to perform the proper functions. But this is not the fault of the Senate. It cannot choose its own members but has to work with what is sent to it. The fault lies back in the citizenship of the states. If the Senate does not function properly the blame is chiefly on them.

If the Vice-President is a man of discretion and character, so that he can be relied upon to act as a subordinate in such position, he should be invited to sit with the Cabinet, although some of the Senators, wishing to be the only advisers of the President, do not look on that proposal with favor. He may not help much in its deliberations, and only on rare occasions would he be a useful contact with the Congress, although his advice on the sentiment of the

[163]

Senate is of much value, but he should be in the Cabinet because he might become President and ought to be informed on the policies of the administration. He will not learn of all of them. Much went on in the departments under President Harding, as it did under me, of which the Cabinet had no knowledge. But he will hear much and learn how to find out more if it ever becomes necessary. My experience in the Cabinet was of supreme value to me when I became President.

It was my intention when I became Vice-President to remain in Washington, avoid speaking and attend to the work of my office. But the pressure to speak is constant and intolerable. However, I resisted most of it. I was honored by the President by his request to make the dedicatory address at the unveiling of a bust of him in the McKinley Memorial at Niles, Ohio. I also delivered the address at the dedication of the Grant statue in Washington.

During these two years I spoke some and lectured some. This took me about the country in travels that reached from Maine to California, from the Twin Cities to Charleston. I was getting acquainted. Aside from speeches I did little writing, but I read a great deal and listened much. While I little realized it at the time it was for me a period of most important preparation. It enabled me to be ready in August, 1923.

An extra session of the Congress began in April of 1921, which was almost continuous until March 4, 1923. While an enormous amount of work was done it soon became apparent that the country expected too much from the change in administration. The government could and did stop the waste of the people's savings, but it could not restore them. That had to be done by the hard work and thrift of the people themselves. This would take time.

While the country was improving it was still depressed. There was some unemployment and a good deal of distress in agriculture because of the very low prices of farm produce and the shrinkage in land values. When I began to make political speeches in the campaign of 1922 I soon realized that the country had large sections that were disappointed because a return of prosperity had not been instantaneous. Moreover the people had little knowledge of the great mass of legislation already accomplished, which was to prove so beneficial to them within a few months in the future. After I had related some of the record of the relief measures adopted they would come to me to say they had never heard of it and thought nothing had been done. While my party still held both the House and Senate it lost many seats in the election, which made the closing session of Congress full of complaints tinged with bitterness against an administration under which many of them had been defeated. That being the natural reaction it is useless to discuss its propriety.

While these years in Washington had been full of interest they were not without some difficulties. Its official circles never accept any one gladly. There is always a certain unexpressed sentiment that a new arrival is appropriating the power that should rightfully belong to them. He is always regarded as in the nature of a usurper. But I think I met less of this sentiment than is usual, for I was careful not to be obtrusive. Nevertheless I could not escape being looked on as one who might be given something that others wished to have. But as it soon became apparent that I was wholly engaged in promoting the work of the Senate and the success of the administration, rather than my own interests, I was more cordially accepted.

In these two years I witnessed the gigantic task of demobilizing a war government and restoring it to a peace-time basis. I also came in contact with many of the important people of the United States and foreign countries. All talent eventually arrives at Washington. Most of the world figures were there at the Conference on Limitation of Armaments. Other meetings brought people only a little less distinguished. While I had little official connection with these events the delegates called on me and I often met them on social occasions.

The efforts of President Harding to restore the country became familiar to me. I saw the steady increase of the wise leadership of Mr. Hughes and Mr. Mellon in the administration of the government and the passing of some of the veteran figures of the Senate. Chief among these was Senator Knox of Pennsylvania. He was a great power and had a control of the conduct of the business of the Senate, which he exercised in behalf of our party policies, that no one else approached during my service in Washington.

In the winter of 1923 President Harding was far from well. At his request I took his place in delivering the address at the Budget Meeting. While he was out again in a few days he never recovered. As Mrs. Coolidge and I were leaving for the long recess on the fourth of March I bade him goodbye. We went to Virginia Hot Springs for a few days and then returned to Massachusetts, where we remained while I filled some speaking engagements, and in July went to Vermont. We left the President and Mrs. Harding in Washington. I do not know what had impaired his health. I do know that the weight of the Presidency is very heavy. Later it was disclosed that he had discovered that some whom he had trusted had betrayed him and he had been forced to call them to account. It is known that this discovery was a very heavy grief to him, perhaps more than he could bear. I never saw him again. In June he started for Alaska and—eternity.

ON ENTERING AND LEAVING
THE PRESIDENCY

CHAPTER FIVE

ON ENTERING AND LEAVING

THE PRESIDENCY

IT is a very old saying that you never can tell what you can do until you try. The more I see of life the more I am convinced of the wisdom of that observation.

Surprisingly few men are lacking in capacity, but they fail because they are lacking in application. Either they never learn how to work, or, having learned, they are too indolent to apply themselves with the seriousness and the attention that is necessary to solve important problems.

Any reward that is worth having only comes to the industrious. The success which is made in any walk of life is measured almost exactly by the amount of hard work that is put into it.

It has undoubtedly been the lot of every native boy of the United States to be told that he will some day be President. Nearly every young man who happens to be elected a member of his state legislature is pointed to by his friends and his local newspaper as on the way to the White House.

My own experience in this respect did not differ from that of others. But I never took such suggestions seriously, as I was convinced in my own mind that I was not qualified to fill the exalted office of President.

I had not changed this opinion after the November elections of 1919, when I was chosen Governor of Massachusetts for a second term by a majority which had only been exceeded in 1896.

When I began to be seriously mentioned by some of my friends at that time as the Republican candidate for President, it became apparent that there were many others who shared the same opinion as to my fitness which I had so long entertained.

But the coming national convention, acting in accordance with an unchangeable determination, took my destiny into its own hands and nominated me for Vice-President.

Had I been chosen for the first place, I could

have accepted it only with a great deal of trepidation, but when the events of August, 1923, bestowed upon me the Presidential office, I felt at once that power had been given me to administer it. This was not any feeling of exclusiveness. While I felt qualified to serve, I was also well aware that there were many others who were better qualified. It would be my province to get the benefit of their opinions and advice. It is a great advantage to a President, and a major source of safety to the country, for him to know that he is not a great man. When a man begins to feel that he is the only one who can lead in this republic, he is guilty of treason to the spirit of our institutions.

After President Harding was seriously stricken, although I noticed that some of the newspapers at once sent representatives to be near me at the home of my father in Plymouth, Vermont, the official reports which I received from his bedside soon became so reassuring that I believed all danger past.

On the night of August 2, 1923, I was awakened by my father coming up the stairs calling my name. I noticed that his voice trembled. As the only times I had ever observed that before were when death had visited our family, I knew that something of the gravest nature had occurred.

His emotion was partly due to the knowledge that a man whom he had met and liked was gone, partly to the feeling that must possess all of our citizens when the life of their President is taken from them.

But he must have been moved also by the thought of the many sacrifices he had made to place me where I was, the twenty-five-mile drives in storms and in zero weather over our mountain roads to carry me to the academy and all the tenderness and care he had lavished upon me in the thirty-eight years since the death of my mother in the hope that I might sometime rise to a position of importance, which he now saw realized.

He had been the first to address me as President of the United States. It was the culmination of the lifelong desire of a father for the success of his son.

He placed in my hands an official report and told me that President Harding had just passed away. My wife and I at once dressed.

Before leaving the room I knelt down and, with the same prayer with which I have since approached the altar of the church, asked God to bless the American people and give me power to serve them.

My first thought was to express my sympathy for those who had been bereaved and after that was done to attempt to reassure the country with the knowledge that I proposed no sweeping displacement of the men then in office and that there were to be no violent changes in the administration of affairs. As soon as I had dispatched a telegram to Mrs. Harding, I therefore issued a short public statement declaratory of that purpose.

Meantime, I had been examining the Constitution to determine what might be necessary for qualifying by taking the oath of office. It is not clear that any additional oath is required beyond what is taken by the Vice-President when he is sworn into office. It is the same form as that taken by the President.

Having found this form in the Constitution I had it set up on the typewriter and the oath was administered by my father in his capacity as a notary public, an office he had held for a great many years.

The oath was taken in what we always called the sitting room by the light of the kerosene lamp, which was the most modern form of lighting that had then reached the neighborhood. The Bible which had belonged to my mother lay on the table at my hand. It was not officially used, as it is not the practice in Vermont or Massachusetts to use a Bible in connection with the administration of an oath.

Besides my father and myself, there were present my wife, Senator Dale, who happened to be stopping a few miles away, my stenographer, and my chauffeur.

The picture of this scene has been painted with historical accuracy by an artist named Keller, who went to Plymouth for that purpose. Although the likenesses are not good, everything in relation to the painting is correct.

Where succession to the highest office in the land is by inheritance or appointment, no doubt there have been kings who have participated in the induction of their sons into their office, but in republics where the succession comes by an election I do not know of any other case in history where a father has administered to his son the qualifying oath of office which made him the chief magistrate of a nation. It seemed a simple and natural thing to do at the time, but I can now realize something of the dramatic force of the event.

This room was one which was already filled with sacred memories for me. In it my sister and my stepmother passed their last hours. It was associated with my boyhood recollections of my own mother, who sat and reclined there during her long invalid years, though she passed away in an adjoining room where my father was to follow her within three years from this eventful night.

When I started for Washington that morning I turned aside from the main road to make a short devotional visit to the grave of my mother. It had been a comfort to me during my boyhood when I was troubled to be near her last resting place, even in the dead of night. Some way, that morning, she seemed very near to me.

A telegram was sent to my pastor, Dr. Jason Noble Pierce, to meet me on my arrival at Washington that evening, which he did.

[177]

I found the Cabinet mostly scattered. Some members had been with the late President and some were in Europe. The Secretary of State, Mr. Hughes, and myself, at once began the preparation of plans for the funeral.

I issued the usual proclamation.

The Washington services were held in the rotunda of the Capitol, followed by a simple service and interment at Marion, Ohio, which I attended with the Cabinet and a large number of officers of the government.

The nation was grief-stricken. Especially noticeable was the deep sympathy every one felt for Mrs. Harding. Through all this distressing period her bearing won universal commendation. Her attitude of sympathy and affection towards Mrs. Coolidge and myself was an especial consolation to us.

The first Sunday after reaching Washington we attended services, as we were accustomed to do, at the First Congregational Church. Although I had been rather constant in my attendance, I had never joined the church.

While there had been religious services, there was

no organized church society near my boyhood home. Among other things, I had some fear as to my ability to set that example which I always felt ought to denote the life of a church member. I am inclined to think now that this was a counsel of darkness.

This first service happened to come on communion day. Our pastor, Dr. Pierce, occupied the pulpit, and, as he can under the practice of the Congregational Church, and always does, because of his own very tolerant attitude, he invited all those who believed in the Christian faith, whether church members or not, to join in partaking of the communion.

For the first time I accepted this invitation, which I later learned he had observed, and in a few days without any intimation to me that it was to be done, considering this to be a sufficient public profession of my faith, the church voted me into its membership.

This declaration of their belief in me was a great satisfaction.

Had I been approached in the usual way to join the church after I became President, I should have feared that such action might appear to be a pose, and should have hesitated to accept. From what might have been a misguided conception I was thus saved by some influence which I had not anticipated.

But if I had not voluntarily gone to church and partaken of communion, this blessing would not have come to me.

Fate bestows its rewards on those who put themselves in the proper attitude to receive them.

During my service in Washington I had seen a large amount of government business. Peace had been made with the Central Powers, the tariff revised, the budget system adopted, taxation reduced, large payments made on the national debt, the Veterans' Bureau organized, important farm legislation passed, public expenditures greatly decreased, the differences with Colombia of twenty years' standing composed, and the Washington Conference had reached an epoch-making agreement for the practical limitation of naval armaments.

It would be difficult to find two years of peacetime history in all the record of our republic that were marked with more important and far-reaching accomplishments. From my position as President of the Senate, and in my attendance upon the sessions of the Cabinet, I thus came into possession of a very wide knowledge of the details of the government.

In spite of the remarkable record which had already been made, much remained to be done. While anything that relates to the functions of the government is of enormous interest to me, its economic relations have always had a peculiar fascination for me.

Though these are necessarily predicated on order and peace, yet our people are so thoroughly law-abiding and our foreign relations are so happy that the problem of government action which is to carry its benefits into the homes of all the people becomes almost entirely confined to the realm of economics.

My personal experience with business had been such as comes to a country lawyer.

My official experience with government business had been of a wide range. As Mayor, I had charge of the financial affairs of the City of Northampton. As Lieutenant-Governor, I was Chairman of the Committee on Finance of the Governor's Council, which had to authorize every cent of the expenditures of the Commonwealth before they could be made. As Governor, I was chargeable with responsibility both for appropriations and for expenditures.

My fundamental idea of both private and public business came first from my father. He had the strong New England trait of great repugnance at seeing anything wasted. He was a generous and charitable man, but he regarded waste as a moral wrong.

Wealth comes from industry and from the hard experience of human toil. To dissipate it in waste and extravagance is disloyalty to humanity. This is by no means a doctrine of parsimony. Both men and nations should live in accordance with their means and devote their substance not only to productive industry, but to the creation of the various forms of beauty and the pursuit of culture which give adornments to the art of life.

When I became President it was perfectly apparent that the key by which the way could be opened to national progress was constructive economy. Only by the use of that policy could the high rates of taxation, which were retarding our development and prosperity, be diminished, and the enormous burden of our public debt be reduced.

Without impairing the efficient operation of all the functions of the government, I have steadily and without ceasing pressed on in that direction. This policy has encouraged enterprise, made possible the highest rate of wages which has ever existed, returned large profits, brought to the homes of the people the greatest economic benefits they ever enjoyed, and given to the country as a whole an unexampled era of prosperity. This well-being of my country has given me the chief satisfaction of my administration.

One of my most pleasant memories will be the friendly relations which I have always had with the representatives of the press in Washington. I shall always remember that at the conclusion of the first regular conference I held with them at the White House office they broke into hearty applause.

I suppose that in answering their questions I had been fortunate enough to tell them what they wanted to know in such a way that they could make use of it.

While there have been newspapers which supported me, of course there have been others which opposed me, but they have usually been fair. I shall always consider it the highest tribute to my administration that the opposition have based so little of their criticism on what I have really said and done.

I have often said that there was no cause for feeling disturbed at being misrepresented in the press. It would be only when they began to say things detrimental to me which were true that I should feel alarm.

Perhaps one of the reasons I have been a target for so little abuse is because I have tried to refrain from abusing other people.

The words of the President have an enormous weight and ought not to be used indiscriminately.

It would be exceedingly easy to set the country all by the ears and foment hatreds and jealousies, which, by destroying faith and confidence, would help nobody and harm everybody. The end would be the destruction of all progress.

While every one knows that evils exist, there is yet sufficient good in the people to supply material for most of the comment that needs to be made.

The only way I know to drive out evil from the country is by the constructive method of filling it with good. The country is better off tranquilly considering its blessings and merits, and earnestly striving to secure more of them, than it would be in nursing hostile bitterness about its deficiencies and faults.

Notwithstanding the broad general knowledge which I had of the government, when I reached Washington I found it necessary to make an extensive survey of the various Departments to acquaint myself with details. This work had to be done intensively from the first of August to the middle of November, in order to have the background and knowledge which would enable me to discuss the state of the Union in my first Message to the Congress.

Although meantime I was pressed with invitations to make speeches, I did not accept any of them. The country was in mourning and I felt it more appropriate to make my first declaration in my Message to the Congress. Of course, I opened the Red Cross Convention in October, which was an official function for me as its President.

I was especially fortunate in securing C. Bascom

Slemp as my Secretary, who had been a member of the House for many years and had a wide acquaintance with public men and the workings of legislative machinery. His advice was most helpful. I had already served with all the members of the Cabinet, which perhaps was one reason I found them so sympathetic.

Among its membership were men of great ability who have served their country with a capacity which I do not believe was ever exceeded by any former Cabinet officers.

A large amount was learned from George Harvey, Ambassador to England, concerning the European situation. He not only had a special aptitude for gathering and digesting information of that nature, but had been located at London for two years, where most of it centered.

I called in a great many people from all the different walks of life over the country. Among the first to come voluntarily were the veteran President and the Secretary of the American Federation of Labor, Mr. Gompers and Mr. Morrison. They brought a formal resolution expressive of personal regard for me and assurance of loyal support for the government.

Farm organizations and business men, publishers, educators, and many others—all had to be consulted.

It has been my policy to seek information and advice wherever I could find it. I have never relied on any particular person to be my unofficial adviser. I have let the merits of each case and the soundness of all advice speak for themselves. My counselors have been those provided by the Constitution and the law.

Due largely to this careful preparation, my Message was well received. No other public utterance of mine had been given greater approbation.

Most of the praise was sincere. But there were some quarters in the opposing party where it was thought it would be good strategy to encourage my party to nominate me, thinking that it would be easy to accomplish my defeat. I do not know whether their judgment was wrong or whether they overdid the operation, so that when they stopped speaking in my praise they found they could not change the opinion of the people which they had helped to create.

I have seen a great many attempts at political strategy in my day and elaborate plans made to encompass the destruction of this or that public man. I cannot now think of any that did not react with overwhelming force upon the perpetrators, sometimes destroying them and sometimes giving their proposed victim an opportunity to demonstrate his courage, strength and soundness, which increased his standing with the people and raised him to higher office.

There is only one form of political strategy in which I have any confidence, and that is to try to do the right thing and sometimes be able to succeed.

Many people at once began to speak about nominating me to lead my party in the next campaign. I did not take any position in relation to their efforts. Unless the nomination came to me in a natural way, rather than as the result of an artificial campaign, I did not feel it would be of any value.

The people ought to make their choice on a great question of that kind without the influence that could be exerted by a President in office.

After the favorable reception which was given to

my Message, I stated at the Gridiron Dinner that I should be willing to be a candidate. The convention nominated me the next June by a vote which was practically unanimous.

With the exception of the occasion of my notification, I did not attend any partisan meetings or make any purely political speeches during the campaign. I spoke several times at the dedication of a monument, the observance of the anniversary of an historic event, at a meeting of some commercial body, or before some religious gathering. The campaign was magnificently managed by William M. Butler and as it progressed the final result became more and more apparent.

My own participation was delayed by the death of my son Calvin, which occurred on the seventh of July. He was a boy of much promise, proficient in his studies, with a scholarly mind, who had just turned sixteen.

He had a remarkable insight into things.

The day I became President he had just started to work in a tobacco field. When one of his fellow laborers said to him, "If my father was President I

[189]

would not work in a tobacco field," Calvin replied, "If my father were your father, you would."

After he was gone some one sent us a letter he had written about the same time to a young man who had congratulated him on being the first boy in the land. To this he had replied that he had done nothing, and so did not merit the title, which should go to "some boy who had distinguished himself through his own actions."

We do not know what might have happened to him under other circumstances, but if I had not been President he would not have raised a blister on his toe, which resulted in blood poisoning, playing lawn tennis in the South Grounds.

In his suffering he was asking me to make him well. I could not.

When he went the power and the glory of the Presidency went with him.

The ways of Providence are often beyond our understanding. It seemed to me that the world had need of the work that it was probable he could do.

I do not know why such a price was exacted for occupying the White House.

GRACE GOODHUE
Before her marriage to Calvin Coolidge

Sustained by the great outpouring of sympathy from all over the nation, my wife and I bowed to the Supreme Will and with such courage as we had went on in the discharge of our duties.

In less than two years my father followed him.

At his advanced age he had overtaxed his strength receiving the thousands of visitors who went to my old home at Plymouth. It was all a great satisfaction to him and he would not have had it otherwise.

When I was there and visitors were kept from the house for a short period, he would be really distressed in the thought that they could not see all they wished and he would go out where they were himself and mingle among them.

I knew for some weeks that he was passing his last days. I sent to bring him to Washington, but he clung to his old home.

It was a sore trial not to be able to be with him, but I had to leave him where he most wished to be. When his doctors advised me that he could survive only a short time I started to visit him, but he sank to rest while I was on my way.

For my personal contact with him during his last

months I had to resort to the poor substitute of the telephone. When I reached home he was gone.

It costs a great deal to be President.

SOME OF THE DUTIES OF
THE PRESIDENT

CHAPTER SIX

SOME OF THE DUTIES OF THE PRESIDENT

AS I recall the mounting events of the years I spent in Washington, I appreciate how impossible it is to convey an adequate realization of the office of President. A few short paragraphs in the Constitution of the United States describe all his fundamental duties. Various laws passed over a period of nearly a century and a half have supplemented his authority. All of his actions can be analyzed. All of his goings and comings can be recited. The details of his daily life can be made known. The effect of his policies on his own country and on the world at large can be estimated. His methods of work, his associates, his place of abode, can all be described. But the relationship created by all these and more, which constitutes the magnitude of the office, does not yield to definition. Like the glory of a morning sunrise, it can only be experienced—it can not be told.

In the discharge of the duties of the office there is one rule of action more important than all others. It consists in never doing anything that some one else can do for you. Like many other good rules, it is proven by its exceptions. But it indicates a course that should be very strictly followed in order to prevent being so entirely devoted to trifling details that there will be little opportunity to give the necessary consideration to policies of larger importance.

Like some other rules, this one has an important corollary which must be carefully observed in order to secure success. It is not sufficient to entrust details to some one else. They must be entrusted to some one who is competent. The Presidency is primarily an executive office. It is placed at the apex of our system of government. It is a place of last resort to which all questions are brought that others have not been able to answer. The ideal way for it to function is to assign to the various positions men of sufficient ability so that they can solve all the problems that arise under their jurisdiction. If there is a troublesome situation in Nicaragua, a General McCoy can manage it. If we have differences with Mexico, a

Morrow can compose them. If there is unrest in the Philippines, a Stimson can quiet them. About a dozen able, courageous, reliable and experienced men in the House and the Senate can reduce the problem of legislation almost to a vanishing point.

While it is wise for the President to get all the competent advice possible, final judgments are necessarily his own. No one can share with him the responsibility for them. No one can make his decisions for him. He stands at the center of things where no one else can stand. If others make mistakes, they can be relieved, and oftentimes a remedy can be provided. But he can not retire. His decisions are final and usually irreparable. This constitutes the appalling burden of his office. Not only the welfare of 120,000,000 of his countrymen, but oftentimes the peaceful relations of the world are entrusted to his keeping. At the turn of his hand the guns of an enormous fleet would go into action anywhere in the world, carrying the iron might of death and destruction. His appointment confers the power to administer justice, inflict criminal penalties, declare acts of state legislatures and of the Congress void, and sit in

[197]

judgment over the very life of the nation. Practically all the civil and military authorities of the government, except the Congress and the courts, hold their office at his discretion. He appoints, and he can remove. The billions of dollars of government revenue are collected and expended under his direction. The Congress makes the laws, but it is the President who causes them to be executed. A power so vast in its implications has never been conferred upon any ruling sovereign.

Yet the President exercises his authority in accordance with the Constitution and the law. He is truly the agent of the people, performing such functions as they have entrusted to him. The Constitution specifically vests him with the executive power. Some Presidents have seemed to interpret that as an authorization to take any action which the Constitution, or perhaps the law, does not specifically prohibit. Others have considered that their powers extended only to such acts as were specifically authorized by the Constitution and the statutes. This has always seemed to me to be a hypothetical question, which it would be idle to attempt to determine in advance. It

would appear to be the better practice to wait to decide each question on its merits as it arises. Jefferson
is said to have entertained the opinion that there was
no constitutional warrant for enlarging the territory
of the United States, but when the actual facts confronted him he did not hesitate to negotiate the Lou-
isiana Purchase. For all ordinary occasions the specific powers assigned to the President will be found
sufficient to provide for the welfare of the country.
That is all he needs.

All situations that arise are likely to be simplified,
and many of them completely solved, by an application of the Constitution and the law. If what they
require to be done, is done, there is no opportunity
for criticism, and it would be seldom that anything
better could be devised. A Commission once came
to me with a proposal for adopting rules to regulate
the conduct of its members. As they were evenly divided, each side wished me to decide against the
other. They did this because, while it is always the
nature of a Commissioner to claim that he is entirely
independent of the President, he would usually welcome Presidential interference with any other Com-

[199]

missioner who does not agree with him. In this case it occurred to me that the Department of Justice should ascertain what the statute setting up this Commission required under the circumstances. A reference to the law disclosed that the Congress had specified the qualifications of the members of the Commission and that they could not by rule either enlarge or diminish the power of their individual members. So their problem was solved like many others by simply finding out what the law required.

Every day of the Presidential life is crowded with activities. When people not accustomed to Washington came to the office, or when I met them on some special occasion, they often remarked that it seemed to be my busy day, to which my stock reply came to be that all days were busy and there was little difference among them. It was my custom to be out of bed about six-thirty, except in the darkest mornings of winter. One of the doormen at the White House was an excellent barber, but I always preferred to shave myself with old-fashioned razors, which I knew how to keep in good condition. It was my intention to take a short walk before breakfast, which Mrs. Coolidge and I ate together in our rooms. For me there was fruit and about one-half cup of coffee, with a home-made cereal made from boiling together two parts of unground wheat with one part of rye. To this was added a roll and a strip of bacon, which went mostly to our dogs.

Soon after eight found me dictating in the White House library in preparation for some public utterance. This would go on for more than an hour, after which I began to receive callers at the office. Most of these came by appointment, but in addition to the average of six to eight who were listed there would be as many more from my Cabinet and the Congress, to whom I was always accessible. Each one came to me with a different problem requiring my decision, which was usually made at once. About twelve-fifteen those began to be brought in who were to be somewhat formally presented. At twelve-thirty the doors were opened, and a long line passed by who wished merely to shake hands with the President. On one occasion I shook hands with nineteen hundred in thirty-four minutes, which is probably my record. Instead of a burden, it was a pleasure and

[201]

a relief to meet people in that way and listen to their greeting, which was often a benediction. It was at this same hour that the numerous groups assembled in the South Grounds, where I joined them for the photographs used for news purposes and permanent mementoes of their White House visit.

Lunch came at one o'clock, at which we usually had guests. It made an opportunity for giving our friends a little more attention than could be extended through a mere handshake. About an hour was devoted to rest before returning to the office, where the afternoon was reserved for attention to the immense number of documents which pass over the desk of the President. These were all cleaned up each day. Before dinner another walk was in order, followed by exercises on some of the vibrating machines kept in my room. We gathered at the dinner table at seven o'clock and within three-quarters of an hour work would be resumed with my stenographer to continue until about ten o'clock.

The White House offices are under the direction of the Secretary to the President. They are the center of activities which are world-wide. Reports come in daily from heads of departments, from distant possessions, and from foreign diplomats and consular agents scattered all over the earth. A mass of correspondence, from the Congress, the officials of the states, and the general public, is constantly being received. All of this often reaches two thousand pieces in a day. Very much of it is sent at once to the Department to which it refers, from which an answer is sent direct to the writer. Other parts are sent to different members of the office staff; and some is laid before the President. While I signed many letters, I did not dictate many. After indicating the nature of the reply, it was usually put into form by some of the secretaries. A great many photographs were sent in to be inscribed, and a constant stream of autographs went to all who wrote for them.

At ten-thirty on Tuesdays and Fridays the Cabinet meetings were held. These were always very informal. Each member was asked if he had any problem he wished to lay before the President. When I first attended with President Harding at the beginning of a new administration these were rather numerous. Later, they decreased, as each member felt better able to solve his own problems. After entire freedom of discussion, but always without a vote of any kind, I was accustomed to announce what the decision should be. There never ought to be and never were marked differences of opinion in my Cabinet. As their duties were not to advise each other, but to advise the President, they could not disagree among themselves. I rarely failed to accept their recommendations. Sometimes they wished for larger appropriations than the state of the Treasury warranted, but they all cooperated most sincerely in the policy of economy and were content with such funds as I could assign to them.

The Secretary of State is the agency through which the President exercises his constitutional authority to deal with foreign relations. As this subject is a matter of constant interchange, he makes no annual report upon it. Other Cabinet officers make annual reports to the President on the whole conduct of their departments, which he transmits to the Congress. All the intercourse with foreign governments is carried on through the Secretary of State, and a national of a foreign country can not be received by the President unless the accredited diplomatic representative of his government has made an appointment for him through the State Department.

All foreign approaches to the President are through this Department. When an Ambassador or Minister is to present his credentials, the Undersecretary of State brings him to the White House and escorts him to the Green Room. After the President has taken his position standing in the Blue Room accompanied by his aides, the diplomat is then brought before him. He presents his letters with a short formal statement, to which the President responds in kind. When the mutual expressions of friendly interest and good will have been exchanged, the accompanying staff of the diplomat is brought in for presentation, after which he retires. Except when foreign officials are presented for an audience in this way, the etiquette of the White House requires that those who are present should remain until the President and the Mistress of the White House retire from the room.

A competent man is assigned from the State Department to have the management of the White

House official social function. He has under him a considerable staff located in one of the basement rooms, known as the Social Bureau. They keep a careful list of all those who leave cards and of the officials who should be invited to receptions, which is constantly revised to meet changing conditions. While the President has supervision over all these functions, the most effective way to deal with them is to provide a capable Mistress of the White House. I have often been complimented on the choice which I made nearly twenty-five years ago. These functions were so much in the hands of Mrs. Coolidge that oftentimes I did not know what guests were to be present until I met them in the Blue Room just before going in to dinner.

These social functions are almost as much a part of the life of official Washington as a session of the Congress or a term of the Supreme Court. The season opens with the Cabinet dinner. Following this come the Diplomatic reception, the Diplomatic dinner, then the Judicial reception, the Supreme Court dinner, then the Congressional reception and the Speaker's dinner, with the last reception of the year tendered to the Army and Navy. About fifty guests assemble at the dinners, except that given to the diplomats, when the presence of the Ambassadors or Ministers, with their wives, of all countries represented in Washington brings the number up to about ninety. The Marine Band is in attendance on all these occasions. Following the dinners a short musical recital by famous artists is given in the East Room, to which many additional guests are invited.

A reception is a particularly colorful event. About thirty-five hundred invitations are issued. When the guests are assembled the President and his wife, preceded by his aides and followed by the Cabinet and his Secretary and their wives, go down the main staircase, pausing for a moment to receive the military salute of the band, and then pass to the Blue Room where the receptions are always held. When the foreign diplomats are present in their official dress, the scene is very brilliant. After all the presentations have been made, the President and his retinue return to the second floor. Immediately after this there is dancing in the East Room to furnish entertainment while the long line of cars comes up to take the guests home.

Whenever the prominent officials of foreign governments visit Washington, it is customary to receive them at a luncheon or dinner at the White House. When the Prince of Wales was here in 1924 we were in mourning, due to the loss of our son, so that he lunched with us informally without any other invited guests. When the Queen of Rumania came to Washington she was entertained at dinner. There have also been Princes of the reigning house of Japan and of Sweden, the Premier of France, the Governor General of Canada, the Presidents of the Irish Free State, of Cuba, and of Mexico, who have been received and entertained in some manner. Whenever an official gathering of foreigners, like the Panama Conference, convenes in Washington, the President and the Mistress of the White House tender them a reception and a dinner.

Besides these formal social gatherings, there were various afternoon teas and musicales, which I sometimes neglected, and usually one or two garden parties held in the South Grounds, one of which was for the disabled veterans who were patients in Washington hospitals. These parties were accompanied with band music and light refreshments, which always seemed to be appreciated by the veterans.

My personal social functions consisted of the White House breakfasts, which were attended by fifteen to twenty-five members of the House and Senate and others, who gathered around my table at eight-thirty o'clock in the morning to partake of a meal which ended with wheat cakes and Vermont maple syrup. During the last session of the Congress I invited all the members of the Senate, all the chairmen and ranking Democratic members of the committees of the House, and finally had breakfast with the officers of both houses of the Congress. Although we did not undertake to discuss matters of public business at these breakfasts, they were productive of a spirit of good fellowship which was no doubt a helpful influence to the transaction of public business.

In addition to these White House events, the President and his wife go out to twelve official dinners. They begin with the Vice-President, go on among the ten members of the Cabinet, and close with the Speaker of the House. Aside from these, it is not customary for the President to accept the hospitality of any individuals. This is not from any desire on his part to be exclusive, but rather arises from an application of the principle of equality. The number of days in his term of office is limited. If he gave up all the time when he is not otherwise necessarily engaged, it is doubtful if he could find fifty evenings in a year when he could accept invitations. At once he would be confronted with the necessity of deciding which to accept and which to reject. If he served eight years, he could only touch the fringe of official Washington, even if he chose to disregard all the balance of the country. The only escape from an otherwise impossible situation is to observe the rule of refusing all social invitations.

The President stands at the head of all official and social rank in the nation. As he is Commander-in-Chief of the Army and Navy, all their officers are his subordinates. As he is the head of the government, he outranks all other public officials. As the first citizen, he is placed at the top of the social scale.

Wherever he goes, whenever he appears, he must be assigned the place of honor. It follows from this that he can not consistently attend a dinner or any other function given by some one else in honor of any other person. He can have ceremonies of his own at the White House, or outside, in which he recognizes the merit of others and bestows upon them appropriate honors. But his participation in any other occasion of such a nature is confined to sending an appropriate message.

It would make great confusion in all White House relations unless the rules of procedure were observed. If this were not done, the most ambitious and intruding would seize the place of honor, or it would be bestowed by favor. In both cases all official position would be ignored. In its working out, therefore, the adoption of rules which take no account of persons, but simply apply to places, is the only method which is in harmony with our spirit of equality. In its application it gives us more completely a government of laws and not of men.

As he is head of the government, charged with making appointments, and clothed with the executive power, the President has a certain responsibility for the conduct of all departments, commissions and independent bureaus. While I was willing to advise with any of these officers and give them any assistance in my power, I always felt they should make their own decisions and rarely volunteered any advice. Many applications are made requesting the President to seek to influence these bodies, and such applications were usually transmitted to them for their information without comment. Wherever they exercise judicial functions, I always felt that some impropriety might attach to any suggestions from me. The parties before them are entitled to a fair trial on the merits of their case and to have judgment rendered by those to whom both sides have presented their evidence. If some one on the outside undertook to interfere, even if grave injustice was not done, the integrity of a commission which comes from a knowledge that it can be relied on to exercise its own independent judgment would be very much impaired.

I never hesitated to ask commissions to speed up their work and get their business done, but if they were not doing it correctly my remedy would be to supplant them with those who I thought would do better. At one time the Shipping Board adopted a resolution declaring their independence of the President and claiming they were responsible solely to the Congress. As I always considered they had a rather impossible task, I doubted whether any one could be very successful in its performance. If they wished to try to relieve me of its responsibility, I had no personal objection and would probably be saved from considerable criticism. But they found they could not carry on their work without the support of the President, so that some of them resigned and the remainder reestablished their contact with the White House, which was always open to them.

The practice which I followed in my relations with commissions and in the recognition of rank has been long established. President Jefferson seems to have entertained the opinion that even the Supreme Court should be influenced by his wishes and that failing in this a recalcitrant judge should be impeached by a complaisant Congress. This brought him into a sharp conflict with John Marshall, who

[213]

resisted any encroachment upon the independence of the Court. In this controversy the position of Marshall has been vindicated. It is also said that at some of his official dinners President Jefferson left all his guests to the confusion of taking whatever seat they could find at his table. But this method did not survive the test of history. In spite of all his greatness, any one who had as many ideas as Jefferson was bound to find that some of them would not work. But this does not detract from the wisdom of his faith in the people and his constant insistence that they be left to manage their own affairs. His opposition to bureaucracy will bear careful analysis, and the country could stand a great deal more of its application. The trouble with us is that we talk about Jefferson but do not follow him. In his theory that the people should manage their government, and not be managed by it, he was everlastingly right.

Tradition and custom, it will be seen, are oftentimes determining factors in the Presidential office, as they are in all other walks of life. This is not because they are arbitrary or artificial, but because long experience has demonstrated that they are the best methods of dealing with human affairs. Things are done in a certain way after many repetitions show that way causes the least friction and is most likely to bring the desired result. While there are times when the people might enjoy the spectacular, in the end they will only be satisfied with accomplishments. The President gets the best advice he can find, uses the best judgment at his command, and leaves the event in the hands of Providence.

Everything that the President does potentially at least is of such great importance that he must be constantly on guard. This applies not only to himself, but to everybody about him. Not only in all his official actions, but in all his social intercourse, and even in his recreation and repose, he is constantly watched by a multitude of eyes to determine if there is anything unusual, extraordinary, or irregular, which can be set down in praise or in blame. Oftentimes trifling incidents, some insignificant action, an unfortunate phrase in an address, an injudicious letter, a lack of patience towards some one who presents an impossible proposition, too much attention to one person, or too little courtesy towards another, become magnified into the sensation of the hour. While such events finally sink into their proper place in history as too small for consideration, if they occur frequently they create an atmosphere of distraction that might seriously interfere with the conduct of public business which is really important.

It was my desire to maintain about the White House as far as possible an attitude of simplicity and not engage in anything that had an air of pretentious display. That was my conception of the great office. It carries sufficient power within itself, so that it does not require any of the outward trappings of pomp and splendor for the purpose of creating an impression. It has a dignity of its own which makes it self-sufficient. Of course, there should be proper formality, and personal relations should be conducted at all times with decorum and dignity, and in accordance with the best traditions of polite society. But there is no need of theatricals.

But, however much he may deplore it, the President ceases to be an ordinary citizen. In order to function at all he has to be surrounded with many safeguards. If these were removed for only a short time, he would be overwhelmed by the people who would surge in upon him. In traveling it would be agreeable to me to use the regular trains which are open to the public. I have done so once or twice. But I found it made great difficulty for the railroads. They reported that it was unsafe, because they could not take the necessary precautions. It therefore seemed best to run a second section, following a regular train, for the exclusive use of the President and his party. While the facilities of a private car have always been offered, I think they have only been used once, when one was needed for the better comfort of Mrs. Coolidge during her illness. Although I have not been given to much travel during my term of office, it has been sufficient, so that I am convinced the government should own a private car for the use of the President when he leaves Washington. The pressure on him is so great, the responsibilities are so heavy, that it is wise public policy in order to secure his best services to provide him with such ample facilities that he will be relieved as far as possible from all physical inconveniences.

It is not generally understood how much detail is

involved in any journey of the President. One or two secret service men must go to the destination several days in advance. His line of travel and every street and location which he is to visit are carefully examined. The order of ceremonies has to be submitted for approval. Oftentimes the local police are inadequate, so that it is necessary to use some of the military or naval forces to assist them. Not only his aides and his personal physician, but also secret service men, some of his office force, and house servants, have to be in attendance. Quarters must also be provided for a large retinue of newspaper reporters and camera men who follow him upon all occasions. Every switch that he goes over is spiked down. Every freight train that he passes is stopped and every passenger train slowed down to ten miles per hour. While all of this proceeds smoothly, it requires careful attention to a great variety of details.

It has never been my practice to speak from rear platforms. The confusion is so great that few people could hear and it does not seem to me very dignified. When the President speaks it ought to be an event. The excuse for such appearances which formerly existed has been eliminated by the coming of the radio. It is so often that the President is on the air that almost any one who wishes has ample opportunity to hear his voice. It has seemed more appropriate for Mrs. Coolidge and me to appear at the rear of the train where the people could see us. About the only time that I have spoken was at Bennington in September of 1928, where I expressed my affection and respect for the people of the state of Vermont, as I was passing through that town on my way back to Washington. I found that the love I had for the hills where I was born touched a responsive chord in the heart of the whole nation.

One of the most appalling trials which confront a President is the perpetual clamor for public utterances. Invitations are constant and pressing. They come by wire, by mail, and by delegations. No event of importance is celebrated anywhere in the United States without inviting him to come to deliver an oration. When others are enjoying a holiday, he is expected to make a public appearance in order to entertain and instruct by a formal address. There are a few public statements that he does not deliver in person, like proclamations, and messages, which go to the Congress, either reporting his views on the state of the Union in his Annual Message or giving his reasons for rejecting legislation in a veto. These productions vary in length. My Annual Message would be about twelve thousand words. My speeches would average a little over three thousand words. In the course of a year the entire number reaches about twenty, which probably represents an output of at least seventy-five thousand words.

This kind of work is very exacting. It requires the most laborious and extended research and study, and the most careful and painstaking thought. Each word has to be weighed in the realization that it is a Presidential utterance which will be dissected at home and abroad to discover its outward meaning and any possible hidden implications. Before it is finished it is thoroughly examined by one or two of my staff, and oftentimes by a member of the Cabinet. It is not difficult for me to deliver an address. The difficulty lies in its preparation. This is an important part of the work of a President which he can not escape. It is inherent in the office.

CALVIN COOLIDGE AND HIS FAMILY
The day he became Governor of Massachusetts

A great many presents come to the White House, which are all cherished, not so much for their intrinsic value as because they are tokens of esteem and affection. Almost everything that can be eaten comes. We always know what to do with that. But some of the pets that are offered us are more of a problem. I have a beautiful black-haired bear that was brought all the way from Mexico in a truck, and a pair of live lion cubs now grown up, and a small species of hippopotamus which came from South Africa. These and other animals and birds have been placed in the zoological quarters in Rock Creek Park. We always had more dogs than we could take care of. My favorites were the white collies, which became so much associated with me that they are enshrined in my bookplate, where they will live as long as our country endures. One of them, Prudence Prim, was especially attached to Mrs. Coolidge. We lost her in the Black Hills. She lies out there in the shadow of Bear Butte where the Indians told me the Great Spirit came to commune with his children. One was my companion, Rob Roy. He was a stately gentleman of great courage and fidelity. He loved to bark from the second-story windows and around the South Grounds. Nights he remained in my room and afternoons went with me to the office. His especial delight was to ride with me in the boats when I went fishing. So although I know he would bark for joy as the grim boatman ferried him across the dark waters of the Styx, yet his going left me lonely on the hither shore.

As I left office I realized that the more I had seen of the workings of the Federal government the more respect I came to have for it. It is carried on by hundreds of thousands of people. Some prove incompetent. A very few are tempted to become disloyal to their trust. But the great rank and file of them are of good ability, conscientious, and faithful public servants. While some are paid more than they would earn in private life, there are great throngs who are serving at a distinct personal sacrifice. Among the higher officials this is almost always true. The service they perform entitles them to approbation and honor.

The Congress has sometimes been a sore trial to Presidents. I did not find it so in my case. Among them were men of wonderful ability and veteran experience. I think they made their decisions with an honest purpose to serve their country. The membership of the Senate changed very much by reason of those who sacrificed themselves for public duty. Of all public officials with whom I have ever been acquainted, the work of a Senator of the United States is by far the most laborious. About twenty of them died during the eight years I was in Washington.

Sometimes it would seem for a day that either the House or the Senate had taken some unwise action, but if it was not corrected on the floor where it occurred it was usually remedied in the other chamber. I always found the members of both parties willing to confer with me and disposed to treat my recommendations fairly. Most of the differences could be adjusted by personal discussion. Sometimes I made an appeal direct to the country by stating my position at the newspaper conferences. I adopted that course in relation to the Mississippi Flood Control Bill. As it passed the Senate it appeared to be much too extravagant in its rule of damages and its proposed remedy. The press began a vigorous discussion of the subject, which caused the House greatly to modify the bill, and in conference a measure that was entirely fair and moderate was adopted. On other occasions I appealed to the country more privately, enlisting the influence of labor and trade organizations upon the Congress in behalf of some measures in which I was interested. That was done in the case of the tax bill of 1928. As it passed the House, the reductions were so large that the revenue necessary to meet the public expenses would not have been furnished. By quietly making this known to the Senate, and enlisting support for that position among their constituents, it was possible to secure such modification of the measure that it could be adopted without greatly endangering the revenue.

But a President cannot, with success, constantly appeal to the country. After a time he will get no response. The people have their own affairs to look after and can not give much attention to what the Congress is doing. If he takes a position, and stands by it, ultimately it will be adopted. Most of the policies set out in my first Annual Message have become law, but it took several years to get action on some of them.

One of the most perplexing and at the same time most important functions of the President is the making of appointments. In some few cases he acts alone, but usually they are made with the advice and consent of the Senate. It is the practice to consult Senators of his own party before making an appointment from their state. In choosing persons for service over the whole or any considerable portion of a single state, it is customary to rely almost entirely on the party Senators from that state for recommendations. It is not possible to find men who are perfect. Selection always has to be limited to human beings, whatever choice is made. It is therefore always possible to point out defects. The supposition that no one should be appointed who has had experience in the field which he is to supervise is extremely detrimental to the public service. An Interstate Commerce Commissioner is much better qualified, if he knows something about transportation. A Federal Trade Commissioner can render much better service if he has had a legal practice which extended into large business transactions. The assertion of those who contend that persons accepting a government appointment would betray their trust in favor of former associates can be understood only on the supposition that those who make it feel that their own tenure of public office is for the purpose of benefiting themselves and their friends.

Every one knows that where the treasure is, there will the heart be also. When a man has invested his personal interest and reputation in the conduct of a public office, if he goes wrong it will not be because of former relations, but because he is a bad man. The same interests that reached him would reach any bad man, irrespective of former life history. What we need in appointive positions is men of knowledge and experience who have sufficient character to resist temptations. If that standard is maintained, we need not be concerned about their former activities. If it is not maintained, all the restrictions on their past employment that can be conceived will be of no avail.

The more experience I have had in making appointments, the more I am convinced that attempts to put limitations on the appointing power are a mistake. It should be possible to choose a well qualified person wherever he can be found. When restrictions are placed on residence, occupation, or profession, it almost always happens that some one is found who is universally admitted to be the best qualified, but who is eliminated by the artificial specifications. So long as the Senate has the power to reject nominations, there is little danger that a President would abuse his authority if he were given the largest possible freedom in his choices. The public service would be improved if all vacancies were filled by simply appointing the best ability and character that can be found. That is what is done in private business. The adoption of any other course handicaps the government in all its operations.

In determining upon all his actions, however, the President has to remember that he is dealing with two different minds. One is the mind of the country, largely intent upon its own personal affairs, and, while not greatly interested in the government, yet desirous of seeing it conducted in an orderly and dignified manner for the advancement of the public

CALVIN COOLIDGE

welfare. Those who compose this mind wish to have the country prosperous and are opposed to unjust taxation and public extravagance. At the same time they have a patriotic pride which moves them with so great a desire to see things well done that they are willing to pay for it. They gladly contribute their money to place the United States in the lead. In general, they represent the public opinion of the land.

But they are unorganized, formless, and inarticulate. Against a compact and well drilled minority they do not appear to be very effective. They are nevertheless the great power in our government. I have constantly appealed to them and have seldom failed in enlisting their support. They are the court of last resort and their decisions are final.

They are, however, the indirect rather than the direct power. The immediate authority with which the President has to deal is vested in the political mind. In order to get things done he has to work through that agency. Some of our Presidents have appeared to lack comprehension of the political mind. Although I have been associated with it for many years, I always found difficulty in understand-

[228]

ing it. It is a strange mixture of vanity and timidity, of an obsequious attitude at one time and a delusion of grandeur at another time, of the most selfish preferment combined with the most sacrificing patriotism. The political mind is the product of men in public life who have been twice spoiled. They have been spoiled with praise and they have been spoiled with abuse. With them nothing is natural, everything is artificial. A few rare souls escape these influences and maintain a vision and a judgment that are unimpaired. They are a great comfort to every President and a great service to their country. But they are not sufficient in number so that the public business can be transacted like a private business.

It is because in their hours of timidity the Congress becomes subservient to the importunities of organized minorities that the President comes more and more to stand as the champion of the rights of the whole country. Organizing such minorities has come to be a well-recognized industry at Washington. They are oftentimes led by persons of great ability, who display much skill in bringing their influences to bear on the Congress. They have ways of securing newspaper publicity, deluging Senators and Representatives with petitions and overwhelming them with imprecations that are oftentimes decisive in securing the passage of bills. While much of this legislation is not entirely bad, almost all of it is excessively expensive. If it were not for the rules of the House and the veto power of the President, within two years these activities would double the cost of the government.

Under our system the President is not only the head of the government, but is also the head of his party. The last twenty years have witnessed a decline in party spirit and a distinct weakening in party loyalty. While an independent attitude on the part of the citizen is not without a certain public advantage, yet it is necessary under our form of government to have political parties. Unless some one is a partisan, no one can be an independent. The Congress is organized entirely in accordance with party policy. The parties appeal to the voters in behalf of their platforms. The people make their choice on those issues. Unless those who are elected on the same party platform associate themselves together to carry out its provisions, the election becomes a mockery. The independent voter who has joined with others in placing a party nominee in office finds his efforts were all in vain, if the person he helps elect refuses or neglects to keep the platform pledges of his party.

Many occasions arise in the Congress when party lines are very properly disregarded, but if there is to be a reasonable government proceeding in accordance with the express mandate of the people, and not merely at the whim of those who happen to be victorious at the polls, on all the larger and important issues there must be party solidarity. It is the business of the President as party leader to do the best he can to see that the declared party platform purposes are translated into legislative and administrative action. Oftentimes I secured support from those without my party and had opposition from those within my party, in attempting to keep my platform pledges.

Such a condition is entirely anomalous. It leaves the President as the sole repository of party responsibility. But it is one of the reasons that the Presidential office has grown in popular estimation and favor, while the Congress has declined. The country feels that the President is willing to assume responsibility, while his party in the Congress is not. I have never felt it was my duty to attempt to coerce Senators or Representatives, or to take reprisals. The people sent them to Washington. I felt I had discharged my duty when I had done the best I could with them. In this way I avoided almost entirely a personal opposition, which I think was of more value to the country than to attempt to prevail through arousing personal fear.

Under our system it ought to be remembered that the power to initiate policies has to be centralized somewhere. Unless the party leaders exercising it can depend on loyalty and organization support, the party in which it is reposed will become entirely ineffective. A party which is ineffective will soon be discarded. If a party is to endure as a serviceable instrument of government for the country, it must possess and display a healthy spirit of party loyalty. Such a manifestation in the Congress would do more than anything else to rehabilitate it in the esteem and confidence of the country.

It is natural for man to seek power. It was because of this trait of human nature that the founders of our institutions provided a system of checks and balances. They placed all their public officers under constitutional limitations. They had little fear of the courts and were inclined to regard legislative bodies as the natural champions of their liberties. They were very apprehensive that the executive might seek to exercise arbitrary powers. Under our Constitution such fears seldom have been well founded. The President has tended to become the champion of the people because he is held solely responsible for his acts, while in the Congress where responsibility is divided it has developed that there is much greater danger of arbitrary action.

It has therefore become increasingly imperative that the President should resist any encroachment upon his constitutional powers. One of the most important of these is the power of appointment. The Constitution provides that he shall nominate, and by and with the advice and consent of the Senate appoint. A constant pressure is exerted by the Senators to make their own nominations and the Congress is constantly proposing laws which undertake to deprive the President of the appointive power. Different departments and bureaus are frequently supporting measures that would make them self-perpetuating bodies to which no appointments could be made that they did not originate. While I have always sought cooperation and advice, I have likewise resisted these efforts, sometimes by refusing to adopt recommendations and sometimes by the exercise of the veto power. One of the farm relief bills, and later a public health measure, had these clearly unconstitutional limitations on the power of appointment. In the defense of the rights and liberties of the people it is necessary for the President to resist all encroachments upon his lawful authority.

All of these trials and encouragements come to each President. It is impossible to explain them. Even after passing through the Presidential office, it still remains a great mystery. Why one person is selected for it and many others are rejected can not be told. Why people respond as they do to its influence seems to be beyond inquiry. Any man who has been placed in the White House can not feel that it is the result of his own exertions or his own merit. Some power outside and beyond him becomes manifest through him. As he contemplates the workings of his office, he comes to realize with an increasing sense of humility that he is but an instrument in the hands of God.

WHY I DID NOT CHOOSE TO RUN

CHAPTER SEVEN

WHY I DID NOT CHOOSE TO RUN

PERHAPS I have already indicated some of the reasons why I did not desire to be a candidate to succeed myself.

The Presidential office takes a heavy toll of those who occupy it and those who are dear to them. While we should not refuse to spend and be spent in the service of our country, it is hazardous to attempt what we feel is beyond our strength to accomplish.

I had never wished to run in 1928 and had determined to make a public announcement at a sufficiently early date so that the party would have ample time to choose some one else. An appropriate occasion for that announcement seemed to be the fourth anniversary of my taking office. The reasons I can give may not appear very convincing, but I am confident my decision was correct.

[239]

My personal and official relations have all been peculiarly pleasant. The Congress has not always done all that I wished, but it has done very little that I did not approve. So far as I can judge, I have been especially fortunate in having the approbation of the country.

But irrespective of the third-term policy, the Presidential office is of such a nature that it is difficult to conceive how one man can successfully serve the country for a term of more than eight years.

While I am in favor of continuing the long-established custom of the country in relation to a third term for a President, yet I do not think that the practice applies to one who has succeeded to part of a term as Vice-President. Others might argue that it does, but I doubt if the country would so consider it.

Although my own health has been practically perfect, yet the duties are very great and ten years would be a very heavy strain. It would be especially long for the Mistress of the White House. Mrs. Coolidge has been in more than usual good health, but I doubt if she could have stayed there for ten years without some danger of impairment of her strength.

A President should not only not be selfish, but he ought to avoid the appearance of selfishness. The people would not have confidence in a man that appeared to be grasping for office.

It is difficult for men in high office to avoid the malady of self-delusion. They are always surrounded by worshipers. They are constantly, and for the most part sincerely, assured of their greatness.

They live in an artificial atmosphere of adulation and exaltation which sooner or later impairs their judgment. They are in grave danger of becoming careless and arrogant.

The chances of having wise and faithful public service are increased by a change in the Presidential office after a moderate length of time.

It is necessary for the head of the nation to differ with many people who are honest in their opinions. As his term progresses, the number who are disappointed accumulates. Finally, there is so large a body who have lost confidence in him that he meets a rising opposition which makes his efforts less effective.

In the higher ranges of public service men appear

to come forward to perform a certain duty. When it is performed their work is done. They usually find it impossible to readjust themselves in the thought of the people so as to pass on successfully to the solution of new public problems.

An examination of the records of those Presidents who have served eight years will disclose that in almost every instance the latter part of their term has shown very little in the way of constructive accomplishment. They have often been clouded with grave disappointments.

While I had a desire to be relieved of the pretensions and delusions of public life, it was not because of any attraction of pleasure or idleness.

We draw our Presidents from the people. It is a wholesome thing for them to return to the people. I came from them. I wish to be one of them again.

Although all our Presidents have had back of them a good heritage of blood, very few have been born to the purple. Fortunately, they are not supported at public expense after leaving office, so they are not expected to set an example encouraging to a leisure class.

They have only the same title to nobility that belongs to all our citizens, which is the one based on achievement and character, so they need not assume superiority. It is becoming for them to engage in some dignified employment where they can be of service as others are.

Our country does not believe in idleness. It honors hard work. I wanted to serve the country again as a private citizen.

In making my public statement I was careful in the use of words. There were some who reported that they were mystified as to my meaning when I said, "I do not choose to run."

Although I did not know it at the time, months later I found that Washington said practically the same thing. Certainly he said no more in his Farewell Address, where he announced that "choice and prudence" invited him to retire.

There were others who constantly demanded that I should state that if nominated I would refuse to accept. Such a statement would not be in accordance with my conception of the requirements of the Presidential office. I never stated or formulated in

[243]

my own mind what I should do under such circumstances, but I was determined not to have that con-
tingency arise.

I therefore sent the Secretary to the President,
Everett Sanders, a man of great ability and discretion, to Kansas City with instructions to notify several of the leaders of state delegations not to vote for
me. Had I not done so, I am told, I should have been
nominated.

The report that he had talked with me on the
telephone after his arrival, and I had told him I
would not accept if nominated, was pure fabrication.
I had no communication with him of any kind after
he left Washington and did not give him any such
instruction or message at any time.

I thought if I could prevent being nominated,
which I was able to do, it would never be necessary
for me to decide the other question. But in order to
be perfectly free, I sent this notice, so that if I declined no one could say I had misled him into sup-
posing that I was willing to receive his vote.

I felt sure that the party and the country were in
so strong a position that they could easily nominate

and elect some other candidate. The events have confirmed my judgment.

In the primary campaign I was careful to make it known that I was not presenting any candidate. The friends of several of them no doubt represented that their candidate was satisfactory to me, which was true as far as it went.

I can conceive a situation in which a President might be warranted in exercising the influence of his office in selecting his successor. That condition did not exist in the last primary. The party had plenty of material, which was available, and the candidate really should be the choice of the people themselves. This is especially so now that so many of the states have laws for the direct expression of the choice of the voters.

A President in office can do very much about the nomination of his successor, because of his influence with the convention, but the feeling that he had forced a choice would place the nominee under a heavy handicap.

When the convention assembles it is almost certain that it will look about to see what candidate has made the largest popular showing, and unless some peculiar disqualification develops it will nominate him.

That was what happened in the last convention, although no one had a majority when the convention assembled.

A strong group of the party in and outside of the Senate made the mistake of undertaking to oppose Mr. Hoover with a large number of local candidates, which finally resulted in their not developing enough strength for any particular candidate to make a showing sufficient to impress the convention.

Although I did not intimate in any way that I would not accept the nomination, when I sent word to the heads of certain unpledged state delegations not to vote for me, they very naturally turned to Mr. Hoover, which brought about his nomination on the first ballot.

The Presidential office differs from everything else. Much of it cannot be described, it can only be felt. After I had considered the reasons for my being a candidate on the one side and on the other, I could not say that any of them moved me with compelling force.

My election seemed assured. Nevertheless, I felt it was not best for the country that I should succeed myself. A new impulse is more likely to be beneficial.

It was therefore my privilege, after seeing my administration so strongly indorsed by the country, to retire voluntarily from the greatest experience that can come to mortal man. In that way, I believed I could best serve the people who have honored me and the country which I love.

THE END